THE ORBIT OF GOD'S LOVE

Prayers & Meditations for Each Day of the Year

AN ANAMCHARA BOOKS SAMPLER

Anamchara Books
Vestal, New York 13850
www.AnamcharaBooks.com

Cover design by Ellyn Sanna.

Paperback ISBN: 978-1-62524-867-1
eBook ISBN: 978-1-62524-868-8

THE ORBIT OF GOD'S LOVE

Prayers & Meditations for Each Day of the Year

AN ANAMCHARA BOOKS SAMPLER

THE ORBIT OF GOD'S LOVE

For the glory of Creation ever streaming from Your heart,
we praise You.
For the air of the eternal seeping through the physical,
we praise You.
For the everlasting glory dipping into time,
we praise You.
For the wonder of Your presence beckoning from each leaf,
we praise You.
For setting us, like the stars in their courses,
within the orbit of Your love,
we praise You.

—Ray Simpson
Dance of Creation

INTRODUCTION

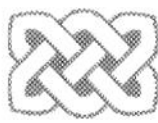

This book contains short selections from thirty-six different titles published by Anamchara Books. In alphabetical order, these are:

All Shall Be Well: A Modern-Language Version of the Revelation of Julian of Norwich by Ellyn Sanna. Julian of Norwich was a medieval mystic whose writing focuses on the meaning of Divine Love.

Become Fire! Guideposts for Interspiritual Pilgrims by Bruce Epperly. Explores the many resources of Christian spirituality in dialogue with the spiritual practices of the world's great wisdom traditions, describing the gifts other spiritual paths contribute to the pathway of Jesus.

Brigid's Mantle: A Celtic Dialogue Between Pagan and Christian by Lilly Weichberger and Kenneth McIntosh. With Brigid, as both a Pagan Goddess and a Christian saint, at the center of their dialogue, the authors describe a Celtic spirituality that embraces the arts, Nature, the supernatural world, compassion for those in need, and gender equality.

Celtic Nature Prayers: Prayers from an Ancient Well edited by Kenneth McIntosh. A collection of prayers expressing the Celtic awareness that Nature is a portal to a deep spiritual reality.

Celtic Prayers and Practices: An Inner Journey by David Cole. Simple and practical meditation techniques from Celtic and other ancient traditions that make use of breath, Nature, scripture, and prayer words.

Celtic Prayers for Times of Crisis compiled by Ellyn Sanna. The prayers collected here, written in the Celtic tradition, offer us ways to spiritually meet the crises of the twenty-first century.

The Celtic Wheel of the Year: Christian & Pagan Prayers & Practices for Each Turning compiled by Meg Llewellyn. Offers readers prayers and seasonal rituals to celebrate the turning year.

From Cosmos to Cradle: Meditations on the Incarnation by Bruce Epperly. Examines the meaning of the Incarnation in our ordinary lives and in the world in which we live.

Dance of Creation: Celtic Prayers of Celebration and Insight, Repentance and Restoration by Ray Simpson. The prayers in this collection ask us to "hear the cry of the earth and work together to 'choose life'" (Deuteronomy 30:19).

Dante's Road: The Journey Home for the Modern Soul by Marc Thomas Shaw. This spiritual guidebook follows in the footsteps of Dante on his journey through the *Divine Comedy*. A fresh, modern take on this classic story.

Deeper: Finding the Depth Dimension Beneath the Surface of Life by Sharon Grussendorff. In the words of Richard Rohr, "written with the clear thinking of a physicist, . . . uses fresh language and creative metaphors to guide the reader on a deepening contemplative journey."

Discovering the Essence: How to Grow a Spiritual Practice When Your Religion Is Cracking Apart by Jeff Campbell. If you're feeling disillusioned with organized religion, this book is for you. Offers ways to access the true essence of spirituality even while you may be questioning or discarding dogmas and doctrines.

Earth Afire with God: Celtic Prayers for Ordinary Life. Prayers and blessings to sanctify daily life, collected and/or written by Anamchara Books' staff.

The Feminine Spirit at the Heart of the Bible by Lynne Bundesen. An insightful reading of the Jewish and Christian scriptures focusing on the feminine, nurturing side of the Divine, ideal for both individual study and groups.

Forest Church: A Field Guide to a Spiritual Connection with Nature by Bruce Stanley. Draws us out, quite literally, into Nature to experience a new, well-thought-through pattern of spiritual practice.

God Online: A Mystic's Guide to the Internet by Bruce Epperly. Each chapter dialogues with a different mystic's writings, calling us to "practice the presence of God" in our online interactions.

Home-Going: The Journey from Racism and Death to Community and Hope by Patrick Saint-Jean, SJ. Uses the lens of African spirituality and the Black experience to call us into a sense of community that extends beyond death into eternity.

Hope in an Age of Fear: Wisdom from the Book of Revelation by Kenneth McIntosh. Explains how the Book of Revelation can be read not as a collection of frightening predictions of the future but as a joyous guide to survival and transformation, even in the face of today's challenges.

I Wonder as I Wander: The 12 Days of Christmas with Madeleine L'Engle by Bruce Epperly. Using the thoughts and words of Madeleine L'Engle, this book offers a joyful guide to Christmas and the days that follow.

Love Prayers from Rumi & Other Sufi Mystics by Devon Holcombe. Modern-language versions of Sufi prayers focusing on the Divine love affair. Includes poems by 11 different Sufi mystics.

101 Soul Seeds for Healing and Wholeness by Bruce Epperly. Each short meditation speaks to the urgent need for both global and personal healing in our time of global crises.

The Peacock's Tail Feathers: Reading the Bible the Celtic Way by Kenneth McIntosh. Learn how the ancient Christian Celts read the Bible and discover new ways to understand the sacred Scriptures today.

Persistent Resistance: Calls for Justice from the Celtic Traditions: A Collection of Essays edited by Ellyn Sanna. Essays from various authors, pointing out the ways in which the Celtic traditions can lead us into mystical experiences of the Divine that must be expressed in acts of justice and tangible compassion.

Prayers of a Christian Sufi by Marietta Bahri Della Penna. Inspired by deep roots in both the Christian and Sufi mystic traditions, this collection of prayers and meditations are honest, tender, and thought-provoking.

Prepare the Way: Celtic Prayers for the Season of Light by Ray Simpson. Prayers that welcome the Holy One who comes to us in small, ordinary ways, who is present in the helpless and the vulnerable.

Repairing the World: The 12 Days of Christmas with Francis and Clare of Assisi by Bruce Epperly. Uses the lives and writings of the saints of Assisi as portals beyond presents and parties into world loyalty and the quest for justice.

Sacred Soil: A Gardener's Book of Reflection by Melina Rudman. A collection of essays that explores the pain of loss and the joy of connection, all within the context of gardening as a spiritual practice.

Santa Claus: Saint, Shaman, and Symbol by Bill Palmer. Explains Santa's history and evolution, from Ice Age shaman to medieval saint to modern-day icon.

Sitting with God: A Journey to Your True Self Through Centering Prayer by Rich Lewis. A practical, friendly, and accessible approach to centering prayer that invites readers into their own spiritual practices.

Song of a Christian Sufi: A Spiritual Memoir by Marietta Bahri Della Penna. Building on the foundations of the Sufi and Christian mystics, a sometimes funny and sometime heartbreaking memoir that always points toward the universal truths beyond the particularities of an individual life.

The Spiritual Work of Racial Justice: A Month of Mediations with Ignatius of Loyola by Patrick Saint-Jean, SJ. Applies Ignatian spirituality to the interior work necessary to deepen our commitment to racial justice.

Thin Places Everywhere: The 12 Days of Christmas with Celtic Christianity by Bruce Epperly. A voyage through the 12 days of Christmas (plus Christmas Eve and Epiphany) with Brendan, Columba, Brigid, Patrick, and other Celtic saints.

Tree of Life: Celtic Prayers to the Universal Christ by Ray Simpson. A collection of original prayers that speak of the wonder, beauty, and love revealed through the Universal Christ, the Tree of Life that includes all that is.

Water from an Ancient Well: Celtic Spirituality for Modern Life: Pilgrim Study Edition by Kenneth McIntosh. Meditates on the "water" that refreshed the ancient Celts, allowing them to perceive God as a living Presence in everybody and everything. (This new version has more than 150 pages of previously unpublished material, including illustrated guides to Celtic pilgrimage sites, study questions, and updated research.)

The Work of Christmas: The 12 Days of Christmas with Howard Thurman by Bruce Epperly. Invites readers to dwell on the meaning of the season in dialog with the wisdom of one of America's greatest mystics and activists, Howard Thurman.

You're Already Home: Kabîr's Vision of the Spiritual Realm by Ellyn Sanna. A modern-language version of the fifteenth-century poet's prayers, expressing the belief that God is within us, woven through both our bodies and our souls.

JANUARY 1

NEW YEAR'S DAY

FACING THE FUTURE WITH GOD

Lord of endless inspiration,
who keeps the seasons turning and creation renewed,
plant in me a renewal of life, as I leave my past behind,
and look forward to what is to come.
Give me the boldness to step out into the future,
knowing that you hold all things in your hand
as I walk the path you lay before me.
May my past not affect me.
May I stand in your righteousness, and move forward
wrapped in the knowledge of a clean heart
and a clear conscience.

—David Cole
Celtic Prayers & Practices

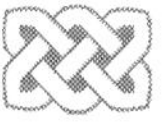

May everything that happens in
the new year ahead, Spirit,
bring me closer to you.

JANUARY 2

BE WITH US

Beloved Ruler of moon and sun and stars,
You know our need,
for You are the merciful God of life.
Each day in this new year,
remind us that we only move
because Your Spirit breathes in us.
Each day in this new year, when we awake,
turn our thoughts to the King of hosts who loves us.
Be with us through each day; be with us through each night.
Be with us each night and day; be with us each day and night.
Be with us through each full moon and each dark moon.
Be with us through sun and storm.
Be with us while the year turns round again.

—Meg Llewellyn
The Celtic Wheel of the Year

Breathe in me, Spirit.

JANUARY 3

CELEBRATION

Divine Birther,
may the whole world celebrate Your existence.
May every person—each gender, each ability,
each colour of skin, and each shape of body—
add to the celebration of Your creation.
May every soul join with the song Nature sings.
May the birds sing, may the trees clap,
and may we humans taste and dance.

—Ray Simpson
Dance of Creation

Show me, Beloved Spirit,
how to join Creation's celebration.

JANUARY 4

CLEAR VISION

Help me see, Divine One.
Remove the scales from eyes.
Show me your light shining forth
from each human being I encounter.
May I look for your presence
in those the world ignores and mistreats.
Teach me to affirm you where you are present,
in each human life.
I have been blind too long.

—Patrick Saint-Jean, SJ
The Spiritual Work of Racial Justice

Help me, Life-Giver,
to see past my stereotypes and prejudices.

JANUARY 5

THE PATH TO SELF

Beloved,
I realize now:
when I keep shouting, "Further on!
I must reach a distant goal!"
I've cut myself off from "here."
I'm living in a fantasy about the future
while I miss the present moment.
When I run back and forth,
looking for a road that leads to future success,
I miss the path
that leads me to my Self.

—Rumi
Love Prayers

Show me your path, Spirit.

JANUARY 6

EPIPHANY

SEEING

High King of the universe,
we offer you our possessions; make them all your own.
We offer you our mindsets
and we place them at your feet.
May we be filled with your Presence
as incense fills a holy place.
We offer you the shadows of our lives,
the things that are crushed;
our little deaths and our final death.
May these be like the straw in the stable,
where Jesus was born.
May something beautiful for you be born in all this straw.
May we see you, as the three Wise Ones did.

—Ray Simpson
The Celtic Book of Days

Holy One, reveal yourself to me today.

JANUARY 7

THE WEB OF BEING

Spirit,
I give thanks
that I am held in a great web of Being,
where the energy of earth and memory,
tree and thought, flower and emotion,
are all knit together
into You.

—Melina Rudman
Sacred Soil

Remind me through this day, Living One,
that I am held, supported, and nourished
by the vast web of your Being.

JANUARY 8

SPIRIT WATER

Jesus proclaims, "Whoever believes in me,
as the Scripture has said, will have streams of living water
flowing from within" (John 7:37).
In Jesus' poetic language, the Holy Spirit is a well
springing forth within us, and the Spirit gives us
what we each need, the Divine Lover
inhabiting our flesh and bones.
Just as water is contained within each human cell—
so that in large part we are water—
so God promises to fill our lives with the Spirit.
Down through the centuries,
people have sought the living water
Jesus described so long ago to the woman at the well.

—Kenneth McIntosh
Water from an Ancient Well

Fill me with, Spirit, with your living water.

JANUARY 9

NEW POSSIBILITIES IN THE MIDST OF CHANGE

Tufwanga mu soba is an African proverb that means:
"We die in order to undergo change."
Death, whether it is our own or a loved one's,
clears an empty space where something new
can come into being and grow.
The African understanding perceives reality
as countless intersecting vibrations,
which send out waves—sometimes small,
like the tiniest ripples on the surface of water,
and sometimes huge, like a tsunami.
When change happens, the literal translation
of what an African would likely say, is,
"My life has been waved (or shaken)."
The larger the wave, the greater the destruction—
and at the same time, the greater the potential
for something radically new to come into being.

—Patrick Saint-Jean, SJ
Home-Going

Life-Giver, show me the hope of new growth,
the fruitful possibilities that will come
out of the changes in my life.

JANUARY 10

CLAIMING THE CROSS

Holy Creator of truth,
kind Creator of mercy,
deliver me from the cold and ice,
deliver me from all evil spells,
deliver me from the charms that would work ill
in my flesh or in my family or in the animals in my care.
Draw Your blessing over this winter day,
draw Your own cross over this winter day,
and on every day;
draw Your cross on my heart this winter night,
and on every night.

—Meg Llewellyn
The Celtic Wheel of the Year

Show me, Creator, how to "draw" the cross of Jesus on this day.

JANUARY 11

THE "REAL" JESUS

We hear a lot about Jesus today,
but the Jesus whose name is used so familiarly—
as though we all know exactly whom we mean—
doesn't seem quite like the Jesus the Celts knew.
Today's Jesus doesn't always shine
with that same lovely light the Celts saw.
And as his followers, we don't always surrender ourselves to him
with the Celts' sense of helpless delight
and incredulous adoration.
As a result, the Christ we think we know
may not seem all that attractive to others.

—Kenneth McIntosh
Water from an Ancient Well

Expand my understanding of Jesus, Beloved One,
beyond what my culture has taught me.

JANUARY 12

THE SPIRITUAL PATH

As many of the mystics recognized,
we rise only through falling.
To come to the land of love,
we have to pass through the pains of death.
We have to do the work of deep recognition.
We have to confront the reality of our suffering,
trace the roots of our harmful patterns,
which usually grow out from our woundedness.
Understanding our particular ego patterns
allows us to live in freedom
and to cultivate compassion more deeply with others.
It enables us to be more present and aware
in the world moment to moment.
It empowers us to go about the work of service in the world.

—Marc Thomas Shaw
Dante's Road

Lead me deeper, Spirit, into the land of love.

JANUARY 13

BEGINNER'S MIND

We best understand God
when we try not to understand God.
This goes back to having a beginner's mind.
We maintain a posture of openness.
We let go and admit that we don't know.
We simply trust. We leave our "small mind"
and enter the "larger mind." We die to our ego.
We die to what the world tells us we need.
We move from "let go" to "let be."
We let ourselves simply "be" with God.

—Rich Lewis
Sitting with God

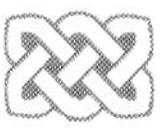

Open my small, self-preoccupied mind, Spirit of Life,
that I might simply be with you.

JANUARY 14

CLOTHED IN THE DIVINE

The Divine Spirit is everything that is good,
everything that comforts us and give us pleasure.
This Spirit is our clothing.
In love, the Divine One wraps us up,
holds us tight, and encloses us with tenderness.
The Spirit lives in everything good that we encounter,
the entire universe,
and we shall never be abandoned.

—Julian of Norwich
All Shall Be Well

Spirit, clothe me in yourself.
Wrap me in your love today.

JANUARY 15

FEAST OF SAINT ITA

THIRSTY FOR GOD

Blessed Ita, who thirsted for God,
may we, like you,
be thirsty for the Bright God, the Giver of Life.
Take hate from our mouths,
remove resentment from our hearts,
and remind us not to place our trust
in the things we can see and touch,
nor in wealth and riches,
but only in the love of the Bright God,
the Giver of All.
Help us to please the Life-Giver
with a firm trust and pure heart.
Teach us to live simply. Remind us to give generously.
Make us thirsty for God.

—Meg Llewellyn
The Celtic Wheel of the Year

Ita was a sixth-century Irish woman
who founded a school,
She was also a healer, a foster mother
to many of the Celtic saints, and a wise counselor.

JANUARY 16

SURRENDER

Beloved One,
I want You to take it all:
my thoughts, feelings, mistakes, heroism, cruelty, beauty,
faithfulness, petty meanness, desires, loves, hates,
emptiness, fullness, loveliness, loneliness,
dreaminess, confusion, hypocrisy, strength, weakness.
Take it all.
If I pretend to be talking about Love, real Love,
what else can I do but surrender it all
to You?

—Marietta Bahri Della Penna
Prayers of a Christian Sufi

Thank you, Beloved,
that you accept everything about me.

JANUARY 17

DORMANCY

My heart lies dormant,
dark and cold like the earth beneath the soil.
Frozen clods cling to my very being,
my deepest sense of my self,
and yet I feel on my face the returning sun.
The Earth's heartbeat is steady,
even in the cold and dark,
confident in the promise of the Spring.

—Meg Llewellyn
The Celtic Wheel of the Year

Keep me steady too, bright Spirit of Light,
even in the cold and dark.

JANUARY 18

THE LONG JOURNEY

You promise me, Beloved God,
that You are here with me, within my very being.
And yet I can only understand You
so slowly, never completely, always indirectly.
When I find enlightenment at last,
I'll say, "Why here You are,
right where You've always been, within my heart!
How could I have been so blind?"
But if I had always seen You here inside me,
I would have never searched for You.
The long journey toward You is the only way
I come to know Your presence.

—Rumi

Love Prayers

Show me yourself, Beloved One.

JANUARY 19

RESTORATION AND HEALING

In every culture and every age,
people have yearned for a world that is "just right."
The experiences of life leave us wishing for somewhere better,
a renewed world where peace and justice reign.
But if there is judgment, its purpose
is to finally remove or purify all evil from the world.
That is to say, God's justice is restorative rather than retributive;
it is designed to heal rather than to punish.

—Kenneth McIntosh

Hope in an Age of Fear

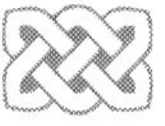

Open me, Spirit, so that I may be
a vehicle of healing and restoration
in the world around me.

JANUARY 20

PRUNING

Imagine if I were a tree,
and my branches were all the many things I am
(or feel I am) responsible for.
Which branches are healthy,
providing me with joy and satisfaction?
How can I invest more in these things?
Which branches can I name that used to be
healthy and joyful, but no longer are?
Can I create an ecosystem so that they still are—
or is it time to let them go?
Which branches are unhealthy, dead,
or rubbing against a branch I want to keep?
How can I give myself permission
to prune these branches from my life?

—Melina Rudman
Sacred Soil

Tree of Life, be the sap in all the branches of my life.

JANUARY 21

EARTH AND BODY

The body has wisdom, and it is a seat of much joy.
The attitude toward the body
is mirrored by the attitude to the Earth.
The same people seeking to leave
the Earth and the body behind
are the types least concerned with catastrophes
like climate change and other forms
of environmental degradation.
How a person feels about the body
Is likely to reflect how they feel about
the whole of the physical world.
Mindfulness is a discipline primarily composed
of practices that are focused on helping people
more fully inhabit their bodies.

—Jeff Campbell
Discovering the Essence

May I always be mindful, Spirit of Life,
that both my body and the Earth's are holy.

JANUARY 22

THE FEMININE SPIRIT

In the original Hebrew of the Book of Genesis,
"Spirit of God," is a feminine noun.
Nothing is said about a bearded old man.
What is said is that the Spirit,
denoted by a feminine word, *moves*.
The Bible tells us at the very beginning:
life springs from the Feminine Spirit.
There is neither a fearsome father
nor an overbearing mother to run from or avoid.
In fact, from this most primordial concept of God,
there is no absent parent for whom to search at all.
There is only Spirit, moving.

—Lynne Bundesen
The Feminine Spirit

Move me, Spirit. Move in me. Move through me.

JANUARY 23

WIDE-OPEN HEARTS

The Celts' passion for Christ did not make them narrow people
mincing their way cautiously through life
lest they fall into sin. On the contrary,
their faith inspired them to open their hearts wider,
to embrace Nature and society more generously,
since they found Christ revealed everywhere
in the everyday world.

—Kenneth McIntosh
Water from an Ancient Well

Expand me, Life-Giver—my thoughts, my understanding,
my perceptions—so that I may see
your Spirit everywhere.

JANUARY 24

TRANSFORMATION

We are not trapped.
Grace extends far beyond our limitations.
From a contemplative perspective,
it's when we reach the end of ourselves
that we are open to encounter
the God who transcends the mental image we've built.
Rather, we encounter the One Who Is,
what the Hebrew scriptures call the I AM.
We do this by entering into silence.
In doing so, we go for a little while beyond the mind
and let go of the concepts we cling to,
allowing even our subconscious
to be subjected to God's transforming presence.
This is where transformation takes place.

—Marc Thomas Shaw
Dante's Road

May even my personal limitations, Life-Giver,
lead me closer to you and to my truest self.

JANUARY 25

FEAST OF SAINT DWYNWEN
(CELTIC LOVERS' DAY)

BUILDING THE HOUSE OF LOVE

Sweet Dwynwen,
you knew both the joy and the pain of love.
We pray for all whose hearts are broken.
We pray for all who love happily and securely.
We pray for lovers to have the strength to love long and well.
Comfort those who sorrow for a lost love.
Give clarity to those who are confused.
Give depth to those who celebrate love's rewards.
In your name, may we always choose love.
In your name and in the name of Christ,
his mother Mary, and Blessed Joseph,
may we, like you, work always to build
the house of love.

—Meg Llewellyn
The Celtic Wheel of the Year

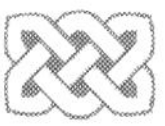

After Dwynwen, a fifth-century Welsh woman,
was separated from her lover,
she prayed God would bless the hopes
and dreams of all true lovers.
She is considered the patron saint
of the brokenhearted.

JANUARY 26

COME OUT AND PLAY!

We get so confused about our role in life.
We think we're here to win a war.
We think it's us against them,
when all along we are here to surrender
more and more deeply to Love.
Sweetheart, run from anything
that could weaken your wings.
Don't listen to anyone
who tries to stab a knife into your awareness
that you are beloved of the Beloved.
I'm not saying you shouldn't be obedient,
but be obedient only to that Voice that's shouting,
"Come out and play with Me."

—Hafiz

Love Prayers

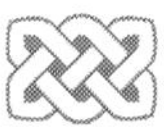

In the midst of life's responsibility and care,
remind me, Beloved, to play with you.

JANUARY 27

A PRAYER FOR USING THE INTERNET

God of technological creativity,
awaken me to your vision of Shalom.
Let your planetary vision guide my interactions
on the Internet and social media,
so that every message glorifies you
and brings truth and beauty to those
with whom I communicate.
Bless my fingers as I type.
Trusting your Loving Wisdom to be
much greater than my own,
may the words of my mouth and meditations of my heart
be acceptable in your sight, O God, my companion,
guide, and inspiration.

—Bruce Epperly
God Online

Each time I look at a computer screen today, Life-Giver,
make me mindful of your presence.

JANUARY 28

FREEDOM

Jesus said, "The truth will set you free."
But what is this truth that will set us free?
I was taught to believe Jesus was talking
about doctrinal truth—and yet it seemed to me,
as I was growing up, that strict doctrine
kept people confined by the need to be right
rather than leading them anywhere near actual freedom.
Doctrine is much more about being right
than it is about being free.
To grow spiritually, we have to want
to be free more than we want to be right.
The truth being referred to in these verses
is an inner truth, a recognition of what goes on
inside us that keeps us stuck.

—Sharon Grussendorff
Deeper

Show me, Spirit of Truth, where am I stuck,
so that I can become free.

JANUARY 29

TIMELESS TIME

The time referred to in the Book of Genesis
as being "in the beginning"
describes Spirit God appearing and acting
through the Cosmos simultaneously.
In my experience, this kind of biblical time is freedom
and endless, perfect peace.
It can reach you, often unpredictably,
wherever you are in chronological o'clock time.

—Lynne Bundesen
The Feminine Spirit

Give me moments in my day, I pray, Life-Giver,
when I dip into the perfect peace
of your timeless time.

JANUARY 30

TRUE REST, TRUE COMFORT

When we perceive the nothingness in reality,
we find God there.
This is why our minds and souls
are often restless and uncomfortable,
because we rely on things that are so small,
which can offer us no real rest or security,
while we fail to realize that the Divine One
is the essence of rest and security, the only true comfort.

—Julian of Norwich
All Shall Be Well

Remind me, Divine One, that only in you
can I find true security and comfort.

JANUARY 31

RACISM WEAKENS US ALL

If one part suffers, all the parts suffer with it
(1 Corinthians 12:26). From this perspective,
racism is neither a "Black problem" nor a "white problem";
it is a killing force within our single shared community.
Racism weakens us all
because it attacks the vital matrix
in which we all live.

—Patrick Saint-John, SJ
Home-Going

Spirit of Love, remind me that racism is a spiritual
as well as social problem.
Give me the courage I need to see clearly,
speak truly, and act in love.

FEBRUARY 1

PRAYER AND ACTION

I want to be engulfed by God's presence, power, and glory.
The only way I can do this is to let go.
I don't really know what God will do
now that God has my full consent.
I want to be in God's Presence. I want to be in God,
and I want God to do whatever God wants.
I consent. This is exciting.
And what God in Christ does with me during my prayer times
will be revealed in the fruits of my actions.

—Rich Lewis
Sitting with God

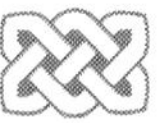

Show me, Spirit of Loving Power,
where I am holding on to things I need to let go.

FEBRUARY 2

SAINT BRIGID'S DAY

THE MANTLE OF PEACE

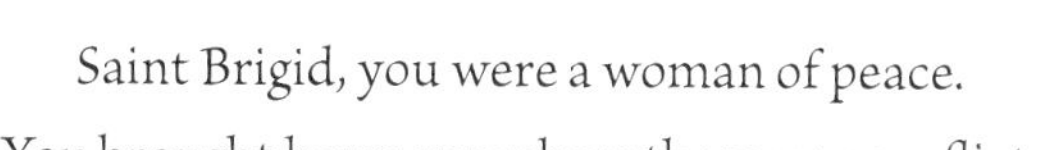

Saint Brigid, you were a woman of peace.
You brought harmony where there was conflict.
You brought light to the darkness.
You brought hope to the downcast.
May the mantle of your peace cover
those who are troubled and anxious,
and may peace be firmly rooted in our hearts
and in our world, on this your holy day.
Inspire us to act justly and to reverence all God has made.
Brigid, you were a voice for the wounded and the weary.
Strengthen what is weak within us.
May we grow this day, and each day
into greater wholeness in mind, body and spirit.

—Kenneth McIntosh
Brigid's Mantle

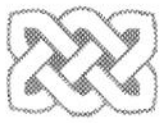

In Celtic tradition, Brigid is both a Pagan goddess and a Christian saint. She represents the threshold between these two spiritualities.

FEBRUARY 3

THE PRESENCE OF BRIGID

On Brigid's Day,
may the bright Goddess's presence
bring you comfort and peace;
may her flame warm your heart and hearth;
may her bright fires inspire
your thoughts, words, and deeds.
May you be forged by your trials
and her strong hand into your most perfect self.
May her cool water heal and sooth your sorrows.
May her mantle protect you from all harm,
and her presence be a light
to guide you through the darkness,
now and always.
Blessed be.

—Lilly Weichberger
Brigid's Mantle

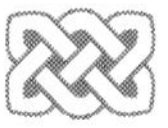

Brigid the Celtic goddess was the
patron of the home fire,
as well as the creative fires of work and inspiration.

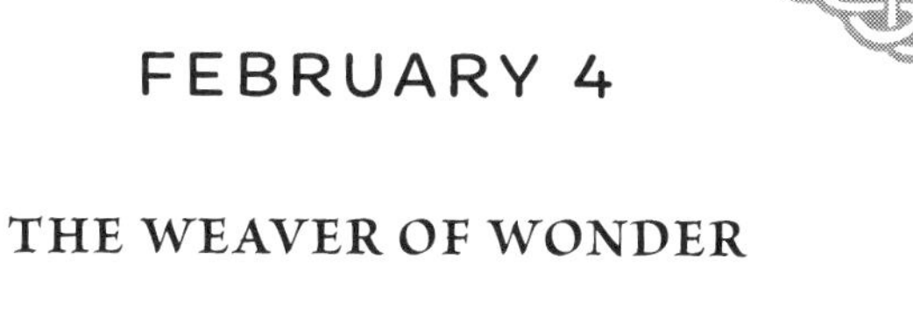

FEBRUARY 4

THE WEAVER OF WONDER

Star-Kindler,
be our light in the cold and darkness.
Weaver of Wonder,
weave in us the patterns of the winter.
Gatherer of souls,
encompass those we see no longer.
Rock of our salvation,
when winter's cold looms large
and icy winds blow hard,
be our warmth and firm foundation.
We draw near to You,
Creator of stars and snow and winter cold,
with our hearts open to Your love
and our minds ready to learn.

—Ray Simpson
Dance of Creation

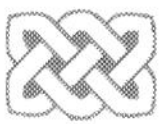

Open my eyes today, Spirit, to your wonder.

FEBRUARY 5

INNER RACISM

I recognize, Holy One,
that racism exists not only in social structures
but also in my own individual thoughts,
attitudes, actions, and inactions.
I ask your forgiveness.
Give me eyes to see into my own heart.
Show me where my priorities need to be reordered.
Dethrone the idol of racism from my soul,
so that I may contribute to the work of antiracism.
Let nothing come between my heart and yours.

—Patrick Saint-Jean, SJ
The Spiritual Work of Racial Justice

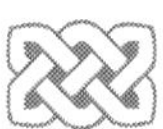

Help me to recognize, Living One,
any prejudice I've hidden within my own heart.

FEBRUARY 6

KNOCK!

"Knock," You say to me,
"and I'll open My door and ask you in.
Disappear,
so you no longer see your own ego,
and I'll make you shine like the sun.
Stumble and fall,
and I'll lift you up to heaven.
Become nothing,
and I'll make you everything."

—Rumi
Love Prayers

Help me, Beloved One,
to no longer worry so much about my ego-self.
Help me to trust you enough
to surrender everything into your hands.

FEBRUARY 7

HOLY FIRE

Lord of the fire,
kindle within me
the passion that drives love,
so that I may live for you with all my strength.
Burn within me with a fire
that consumes my whole being.
Engulf me in your Holy Fire
that falls from heaven into the center of my being.
Kindle the flame within my heart, Lord,
that it might ignite others
whose lives touch mine.

—David Cole
Celtic Prayers & Practices

Kindle me, Holy Fire,
so that my heart is filled with light.

FEBRUARY 8

EGO HABITS

The wisdom traditions teach
that before new life can begin,
a death is always required.
We can't escape the prison of addiction and selfishness
until we die to our habitual ways of being.
We must die to our normal understanding of who we are
for change to occur, for healing to begin,
for love to become possible.

—Marc T. Shaw
Dante's Road

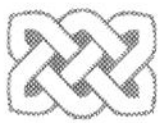

Reveal to me, Spirit of Vision,
any habitual ways of being
that are holding me back from love and healing.

FEBRUARY 9

GOD-IN-A-BOX

Too often our concepts of God
were handed to us within a tightly wrapped box.
We inherit the God passed along to us,
a God who has been neatly defined for us.
We interact with this concept in various ways,
at various levels of comfort, but wonder, delight, and passion
are often missing from those interactions.
Ultimately, the world around us may seem
far more present and real
than even our most devoutly held religious beliefs.
Modern Christianity exerts a lot of intellectual energy,
analyzing and examining the doctrinal foundations of the faith.
We sometimes neglect, however, to
involve our bodies and emotions,
as the ancient Celts did in their love affair with the Divine.

—Kenneth McIntosh
Water from an Ancient Well

Life-Giver, smash the mental box I've kept you in,
so that I can fall in love with you, body, mind, and soul.

FEBRUARY 10

THE POWER OF LOVE

I used to believe that my love
could change the laws of physics;
that it would somehow multiply loaves and fishes
if only I were intent enough.
I used to believe that my love
could protect my loved ones from pain and suffering.
I used to believe that love was a force,
but that disbelief is a temptation.
Now I know that love is only a power,
not a power over, not a power to change what is
into what I want it to be.
Instead, it is a power to create space
for what needs to emerge.
Only that, and yet, as painful as that can be,
is the power of creation itself.

—Melina Rudman
Sacred Soil

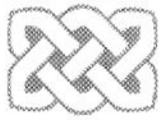

May my love—like yours, Beloved—never seek to control.

FEBRUARY 11

WOMAN AND THE EARTH

After gender and sex
are introduced into biblical accounts,
attacks are made on the "seed of the woman."
The question we can ask is this:
are these attacks on woman only—
or are they also attacks on the Spirit and Creation?
As we trace the word "seed" through the Bible,
the answer seems clear to me:
woman and the Earth are intertwined
within scriptural symbolism, and both
have been assaulted and wounded
by a patriarchal society.

—Lynne Bundesen
The Feminine Spirit

Show me ways, Divine Spirit, that I can participate in fighting the death-dealing patterns of patriarchy.

FEBRUARY 12

GOD ONLINE

Given how much time
many of us spend on social media,
the quality of our spiritual lives depends
on bringing our highest selves to our Internet interactions.
God's intimate presence in our lives invites us
to consider the sacramental nature of social media.
We need to bring the better angels of our nature
to every encounter, whether in the marketplace or online.
Is it possible for us to make the Internet
a temple of the Holy Spirit,
a sacrament of words and images?

—Bruce Epperly
God Online

May your Spirit, Life-Giver, take shape
in every interaction of my life,
including the ones that take place online.

FEBRUARY 13

SPACIOUSNESS

The perspective the Spirit brings
offers us a much more expansive view of our lives,
one that yields a spaciousness
that's free from the old restrictions
we've placed on ourselves.
Those old mental habits no longer need
to restrict our inner sense of abundance,
well-being, and freedom.
A key way to grow our awareness
of this expansive view is through times
of quiet, open, and receptive listening
for the vast and mysterious ways of God.

—Sharon Grussendorff
Deeper

Lead me, Spirit, into your spacious
awareness and freedom.

FEBRUARY 14

VALENTINE'S DAY

LOVE AND IDENTITY

Love is woven into our very identities,
before we were even born.
We came into this world from God;
in God, we live and move and have our being (Acts 17:28).
At the end of our lives, we return to God—
and in the meantime, every beat of our hearts,
every breath we take, every drop of water we swallow,
and every photon that brings light to our world
comes to us as an expression of God's love.

—Kenneth McIntosh
Water from an Ancient Well

Beloved, reveal yourself and your love to me
in each ordinary moment of today.

FEBRUARY 15

THE BODY

The question of "What do I do with this body?"
is a deeply spiritual question.
Some people might try to diminish
and downplay our physicality.
They might even do it with a veneer of religiosity.
As we seek the essence of spirituality, however,
we find something rather surprising.
We find that the body is the doorway
to embracing the world that we are already occupying.
The body's physical senses are the ways
we find out some important things
about how to be in the world. How to feel content.
How to occupy the present moment.
How to appreciate so much beauty
that would have gone unnoticed.

—Jeff Campbell
Discovering the Essence

Thank you, Living One, for my body.
May I honor and celebrate its wonder.

FEBRUARY 16

THE COMMUNITY OF LIFE

In the New Testament Epistles,
the word "you" is usually plural
The ancient Celts provide a healthy model
of reading the Bible from the perspective of "you-all"—
a community of individuals
in vital and intimate relationship
with one another, across both time and space.

—Kenneth McIntosh
The Peacock's Tail Feathers

Remind me, Spirit of Love, that your ways
always extend beyond me to include
the entire living network of community.

FEBRUARY 17

WAKING UP

When you're asleep,
you often don't know you're asleep,
you don't know you're dreaming,
and it came to me now that I had to become aware
of all the ways I'd been asleep for most of my life.
The process wasn't easy, like when a limb
that's been asleep regains feeling:
it feels worse before it feels better.
I stumbled and fell.
I'd think I had everything all figured out—
and then I'd fall again.
But the voice pulling me forward
refused to be silent.

—Marietta Bahri Della Penna
Song of a Christian Sufi

Wake me up, Spirit.
Pull me forward into something new.

FEBRUARY 18

DIVINE DIVERSITY

God delights in diversity.
Diversity characterizes the creative processes
that give birth to a wondrous variety
of belief systems, cultures, rituals, races,
and personality types, not to mention the myriad genus,
species, flora, and fauna that populate the Earth
and the cosmos from which our planet emerged.
The spiritual landscape is also dynamic, diverse, and evolving.
Yes, God delights in diversity.

—Bruce Epperly
Become Fire!

May I too celebrate diversity, Spirit of Life,
rather than being threatened by it.

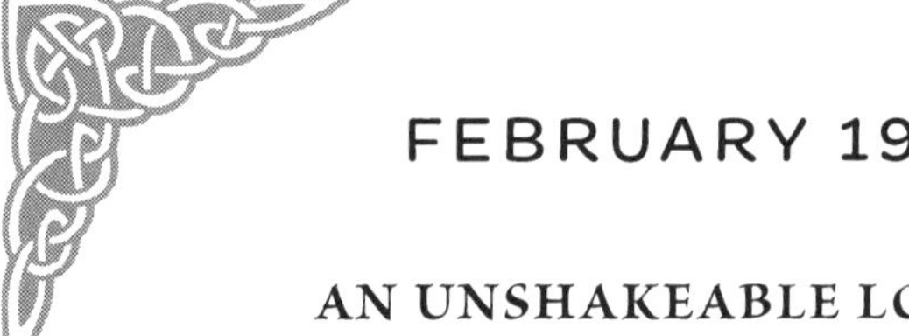

FEBRUARY 19

AN UNSHAKEABLE LOVE

In our ignorance and incomprehension of love,
we use many methods to ask God for what we want.
But I realized that God is worshipped—and delighted—
when we simply turn to the Divine One,
trusting totally in the Unity of God
and clinging to Divine grace.
This attitude reveals a deeper understanding of God
and creates in us an unshakeable love,
far more than any method of prayer our minds could contrive.
Focusing our attention on the absolute Unity
that is never severed, we achieve the truest form of prayer.

—Julian of Norwich
All Shall Be Well

Help me, God of Love, to trust you more.
I want your love to hold me steady.

FEBRUARY 20

FROM THE STARS

The word desire has its roots in *de sidere*—"from the stars."
Our desire for a spiritual home is a celestial guiding force,
similar to the way in which navigators
once relied on the stars for direction.
On Dante's journey through Hell, purgatory,
and paradise in the Divine Comedy,
he is constantly looking up at the stars, drawn to the heavens,
oriented by them on his upward journey toward God.
This profound longing is what the various wisdom traditions
call spiritual hunger . . . the movement toward union with God,
the ultimate goal of the spiritual journey.

—Marc T. Shaw
Dante's Road

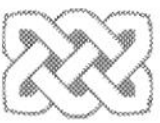

Show me the "stars"—the desires and longings—
I can use, Spirit, to guide my journey.

FEBRUARY 21

NOW

Where are you looking for Me?
Look! I'm right here! I'm right beside you!
But you will not find Me in churches or mosques;
I am not in cathedrals or on holy mountains,
nor am I in rites and ceremonies,
prayers and self-denial.
If you really want to seek Me,
the only place you will find me is—
NOW
in this moment, in this breath,
for I am the Breath that breathes through all breath.

—Kabîr

You're Already Home

May I remember today, Spirit,
to seek you in each moment.

FEBRUARY 22

THE DIVINE PLAN

Humans can choose to live in alienation
from God, from each other, from Nature,
and even from our own true essence.
Our egoic striving quenches community,
and then strife replaces mutual concerns.
Driven by greed, we produce more and more,
exhausting the world's power to renew
and drowning ourselves in an abyss
of unsustainable consumption.
But God's plan for the world
is that all of humanity and all other creatures
share in one beloved community.

—Kenneth McIntosh
Hope in an Age of Fear

Divine Friend, help me to choose the way of community,
rather than the path of alienation.

FEBRUARY 23

BENEATH THE WAVES

Imagine the sea's wild waves are breaking over you.
If you stay on the waves' surface level,
you may quickly become overwhelmed—
but if you dive deeper, beneath the turbulent water,
you'll find that everything is peaceful and quiet,
and the waves lose their threat.
This process of diving deeper is like our journey into God:
beneath the surface of life,
we discover the vast freedom of God,
where we are held, loved, and kept ultimately secure.
This movement has been described
as falling through our lives' *circumstances*
into our real lives—expansive, liberated,
filled with joy, hope, and love.

—Sharon Grussendorff
Deeper

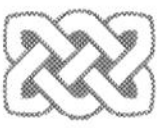

Living One, I want to dive deeper into your reality.

FEBRUARY 24

GOD KNOWS WHAT YOU NEED

God can fill us with whatever She feels we need.
We might be filled with love, peace,
or mental and physical healing.
We might be filled with sudden needed knowledge
to accomplish our daily tasks or with an urge to serve.
We might be moved to make a major shift
in our personal and work life or nudged to try something new.
We might be asked to make a call
to repair an estranged relationship
or sit and listen to someone in pain
who needs a hug and an attentive ear.

—Rich Lewis
Sitting with God

Fill me, Mother God, with whatever I truly need.

FEBRUARY 25

GOD MOVES THROUGH ALL THINGS

The heart of spirituality involves lovingly embracing
God and all things. God speaks to us in gentle winds,
warms us with passionate fire,
serenades us with the hymns of sparrows,
and heals us with compassionate touch.
For Francis, the skin of lepers became sacramental,
and all creation praises God,
because God moves through all things—
body, mind, spirit, relationships.
Heaven and earth jointly declare God's glory.
We may turn from God, preferring the self-centered desires
of our own hearts, but the Light always turns toward us.

—Bruce Epperly
From Cosmos to Cradle

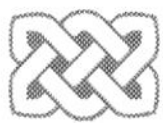

May I sense your movement in all things, Spirit of Light.

FEBRUARY 26

HOPE AND HEALING

Hope goes hand in hand with healing.
Healing brings wholeness to what is broken.
It doesn't reverse the crisis;
it doesn't undo the catastrophe.
Instead, it rises out of crisis, giving meaning
to even the worst circumstances.
In the midst of danger and hardship,
healing brings to life new strengths,
creating something larger and better
than we could ever have dreamed.

—Ellyn Sanna
Celtic Prayers for Times of Crisis

In the midst of my life's crises, Life-Giver,
bring hope and healing.

FEBRUARY 27

ABUNDANCE

Abundance is a feminine concept
that threads throughout the Bible.
The prophet promises, "For you will nurse and be satisfied
at her comforting breasts; you will drink deeply
and delight in her overflowing abundance,"
while the psalmist writes, "They feast
on the abundance of your house."
This theme extends into the Christian New Testament,
where the Greek for "abundance" speaks of
the generosity, potency, bounty, and fruitfulness
that continues to flow out from God to humankind.
In the Bible, no virtue is gained nor points awarded
for starvation or privation, either physical or emotional.

—Lynne Bundesen
The Feminine Spirit

Today, Spirit, may I experience and
celebrate your abundance.

FEBRUARY 28

THE SURRENDER OF LOVE

O Life-Giver,
teach me to love as You do,
without condition,
without insisting on my way.
Let my love make room
for whatever needs to come forth,
whether it be dark or light,
sorrow or joy.
Teach me to surrender
to love's true power.

—Melina Rudman
Sacred Soil

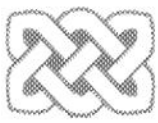

May love break open my shut doors and closed boxes,
so that I may grow.

FEBRUARY 29

LEAP DAY

AN ENLARGED GAZE

In the Gospels, we meet Jesus,
the human manifestation of the Divine,
and in the Book of Revelation, our gaze is enlarged
to encompass the Cosmic Christ,
who is always everywhere and in everything.
Religion may divide people,
but Christ is the reality of all beings' oneness,
the Divine Light that energizes whales and electrons,
galaxies and neurons, the elements and flora and fauna
of existence throughout the universe.
Gazing at the Cosmic Christ in John's Apocalypse,
we catch a glimpse of a greater, all-inclusive perspective.

—Kenneth McIntosh
Hope in an Age of Fear

Shatter my assumptions about you, Spirit of Love,
so that I can catch a glimpse of your limitless reality.

MARCH 1

SAINT DAVID'S DAY

LITTLE THINGS

Giver of Life,
I ask that you help me to be joyful
even in the midst of frustration,
even in discouragement, even in sorrow.
Give me strength
to remain faithful to love, steadfast in hope.
I ask you not for the ability to do great things,
but only that I may keep on doing little things,
one by one, that demonstrate Your love.
Giver of Life, this I ask you
that I may be joyful and faithful,
and continue doing the little things
You give to me to do.

—Meg Llewellyn
The Celtic Wheel of the Year

On his deathbed on March 1, 587, David, the patron saint of Wales, said: "Be joyful, brothers and sisters. Keep your faith, and do the little things."

MARCH 2

THE TRUE SELF

The self we seek is dynamic, multidimensional,
and constantly growing.
Divine energy flows in and through us.
Opening to God's energy within us
widens and deepens our lives
and gives us perspective on life's challenges.
Look inside yourself.
Listen to your evolving life.
Embrace your connectedness with all creation.
And then, let your life speak!

—Bruce Epperly
101 Soul Seeds of Healing and Wholeness

Spirit, let your life enliven, enlighten, and energize me.
Let me experience my grandeur as
well as my imperfection,
trusting that you have a vision of greatness for me.

MARCH 3

DEEPER!

I've been walking along the edge of the ocean,
my pants rolled up to keep them dry.
Now I'm ready
to strip off all my clothes
and dive naked into You.
I want to go beneath the surface,
deeper and deeper,
a thousand times deeper!

—Rumi
Love Prayers

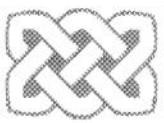

Help me, Spirit,
to not be afraid of your depths

MARCH 4

EXPANDED IDENTITIES

When we cling to what is good for us alone,
both as a society (or nation) and as individuals,
we find ourselves in competition with those around us
for money, attention, power, affection, and control.
Even if we expand our sense of identity
beyond our individual interests and
invest it into our community—
or tribe or church or organization—
we often cling to our sense of pride in our separation,
our differences, our so-called superiority.
We prove to ourselves over and over
that we're right and they're wrong.
Our spiritual journey requires that we unearth
and examine the distortions within our own hearts and minds.
Rooted in awareness of ourselves,
we can contribute more effectively to peace and wholeness.

—Marc Thomas Shaw
Dante's Road

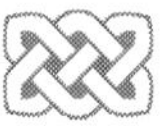

Give me courage, Beloved Spirit, to
examine my own selfishness,
in order to build a more just world.

MARCH 5

THE LABYRINTH OF LOVE

Loving God is a lifelong pilgrimage, a labyrinth walk
that in this mortal life never fully reaches the center point.
We may have occasional, intense experiences of Divine love,
but ordinary life is generally not lived on
the emotional mountaintops.
This is only normal. We shouldn't feel guilty or beat ourselves up
if our passion for God rises and falls from day to day.
As all long-married lovers know,
that is the role of commitment:
to carry us even when our emotions seem to flag,
knowing that sooner or later our passion will surge again.

—Kenneth McIntosh
Water from an Ancient Well

Hold me steady, Beloved Spirit,
through the daily rise and fall of my emotions.

MARCH 6

RESTING IN THE UNITY OF GOD

Resting in the Divine Unity brings our souls to life;
it brings us more of life's fullness;
and our lives expand with grace and strength.
This attitude of prayer aligns most easily with our very natures,
and it requires the least effort to achieve,
for it is simply what our souls already crave,
and what they shall always crave
until we truly understand
that we are wrapped in the Divine Unity:
the goodness of God.

—Julian of Norwich
All Shall Be Well

Bring me to life with your love, Beloved.
Expand my identity with your grace.
Wrap me in your Spirit.

MARCH 7

THE SPIRITUAL CHALLENGE OF SOCIAL MEDIA

What would it be like to approach our social media
and Internet interactions
as consecrated for service and healing?
Can you imagine someone whose political and social
viewpoints differ from your perspective
as a manifestation of the Spirit?
Can you imagine Divine light, peeking out from persons
who perpetuate fake news and incivility?
Can you seek holiness
disguised by offensive political affiliations?

—Bruce Epperly
God Online

Teach me, Spirit of Love, to see you,
even in the unlovely.

MARCH 8

THE ARK OF GOD

The animals are brought into the Ark
as both males and females;
and the Ark is lifted above the earth on the waters—
the same waters upon which the Feminine Spirit
moved in the first chapter of Genesis.
This Spirit also moves the Ark and its inhabitants.
The Ark represents safety and security,
a place evil and danger cannot reach.
It's a feminine word in Hebrew,
And the Ark's purpose is much like a woman's womb.
Both carry life and keep it safe
until conditions are ripe for it to emerge.

—Lynne Bundesen
The Feminine Spirit

When life is stormy, Spirit, carry me in your Ark.

MARCH 9

FLESH AND BONE

I don't have to choose between
embracing my physical presence
and longing for spiritual fullness.
There is value in me sitting with a tension
rather than trying to resolve it.
It might even be that I will most fully experience one
by embracing the other.
If I enter into the physical particularities of my life
this very moment on planet Earth,
lived, as it is in imperfect body,
if I accept and celebrate this here and now,
I find out something new about my hopes
that live beyond this flesh.

—Jeff Campbell
Discovering the Essence

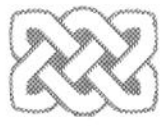

Reveal your Spirit to me, I pray,
through my very flesh and bones.,

MARCH 10

THE GATE OF HEAVEN

So much of the time we are unaware,
asleep to the living Presence of God.
The religious orientation in which many of us grew up
focused on our *ideas* about God
and about right and wrong.
When we try to be religious, we reflect on these ideas—
but we miss the *experience* of knowing God.
Our religion is theological and moral,
rather than experiential.
Meanwhile, God is in *this* place, in *this* time;
this very moment is the gate of heaven.

—Sharon Grussendorff
Deeper

I don't want to be "religious," Spirit of Love;
I want to be in an intimate relationship with you.

MARCH 11

THE CREATOR

The creature is in the Creator,
and the Creator is in the creature:
they are ever distinct, yet ever united.
The Creator is the tree, the seed, and the embryo.
The Creator is the flower, the fruit, and the shade.
The Creator is the sun, the light, and the lighted.
The Creator is both God and creature
and the illusion our eyes perceive.
The Creator is manifold in form, infinite in space;
God is the breath, the word, and the meaning.

—Kabîr
You're Already Home

May I see you, Living One, in each thing, each person, each emotion, and each thought.

MARCH 12

THE LIGHT

All of us are God's children, God's beloved,
Receiving God's enlightenment.
We are awesome and miraculous in the intricacies
of our bodies, minds, and spirits.
Those who turn to the Light, letting it shape their lives,
are given the power to become children of God—
in other words, fully experience
the energy of love in their lives.
Filled with God's spirit, they can do great things
and transform the world.
The Light shines in them, inspiring them
to be God's lights in the world.

—Bruce Epperly
From Cosmos to Cradle

Shine in me, Spirit of Light.

MARCH 13

THE MEANING OF "ECO-SPIRITUALITY"

Take a long, contemplative "look"
at your home and its ecosystems.
Where does human convenience compromise
the lives of other creatures?
Let yourself have feelings about this;
notice what those feelings are.
How might you become more aware
of the lives around your life?
What have you seen for so long that you no longer see it?
What sounds do you no longer hear?
When does your busy-ness overrun your kindness?
What is your best mindfulness practice to counter this?

—Melina Rudman
Sacred Soil

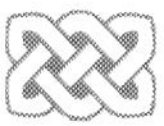

Show me, Creator, ways I can honor your Creation with greater consistency and integrity.

MARCH 14

LETTING GO IN PRAYER—AND IN LIFE

When we incorporate silence into our day,
the day is transformed. Silence is a time when we let go
and let God work in us. Why is this so important?
Because "letting go" during silent prayer
is merely practice for the "letting go" that must continue
during our daily lives. We need this continuity
if we truly want to see, live, and experience abundant life.
We let go of our pet project
and check in with our spouse about her hard day.
We set aside our all-consuming online work
to start the cherished nerf-gun battle with our eight-year-old.
We let go of our exciting plans for the day
and visit our friend struggling with sobriety.

—Rich Lewis
Sitting with God

Help me, Beloved One, to let go of anything
that comes between me and others in my life,
as well as between me and you.

MARCH 15

RAINBOW OF PROMISE

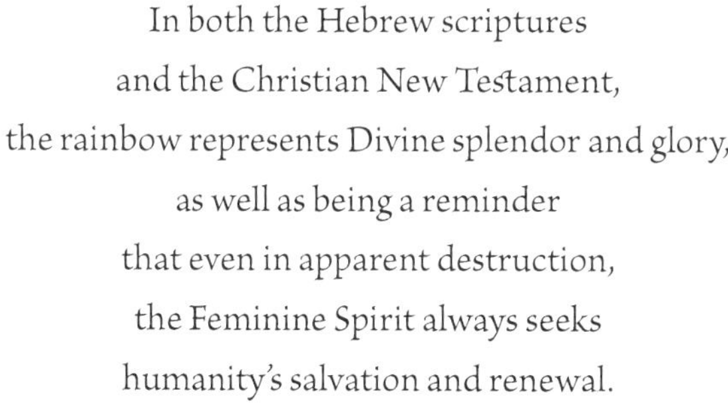

In both the Hebrew scriptures
and the Christian New Testament,
the rainbow represents Divine splendor and glory,
as well as being a reminder
that even in apparent destruction,
the Feminine Spirit always seeks
humanity's salvation and renewal.

—Lynne Bundesen
The Feminine Spirit

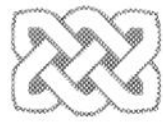

Open my eyes to your "rainbows," Spirit;
remind me that your light and splendor
always work to heal and save.

MARCH 16

OLD OPERATING SYSTEMS

Early in childhood, we all developed strategies
to cope with pain and our sense of lack.
At the same time, we absorbed the additional layers
of family and cultural conditioning.
These thought patterns become so deeply ingrained
as to be nearly invisible to us.
On the surface, we may consider ourselves
to be enlightened, progressive, compassionate people,
never realizing that we are all the while functioning
with an old operating system.

—Marc Thomas Shaw
Dante's Road

Reveal to me, Spirit of Truth,
any old operating systems that are limiting my life.

MARCH 17

SAINT PATRICK'S DAY

STRENGTH!

I arise today
through the strength of the love of cherubim,
in the obedience of angels, in the service of archangels.
I arise today, through the strength of heaven,
the light of the sun, the radiance of the moon,
the splendor of fire, the speed of lightning,
the swiftness of wind, the depth of the sea,
the stability of the earth, the firmness of rock.
I arise today, through
God's strength to pilot me, God's might to uphold me,
God's wisdom to guide me, God's eye to look before me,
God's ear to hear me, God's word to speak for me,
God's hand to guard me, God's shield to protect me,
God's host to save me.

—attributed to Saint Patrick
The Celtic Wheel of the Year

May I learn, Life-Giver, to draw on the strength offered me by all Creation.

MARCH 18

BE THOU MY VISION

God is as close as our own heartbeat,
with us while we are "waking or sleeping."
God is there in our "best thoughts" and our truest words;
The Divine Presence is always with us, a shelter for our souls,
while at the same time dwelling within us,
the "great Heart" of our own hearts,
that which gives us both dignity and delight.
In the Divine Presence, "we live and move
and have our existence" (Acts 17:28).
We can see God everywhere;
God is our vision.

—Kenneth McIntosh
Water from an Ancient Well

May I, Life-Giver, like the author of the ancient hymn, "Be Thou My Vision," seek your presence everywhere.

MARCH 19

KNOW THEIR NAMES

Jesus, make real to me the sorrow of your death.
May I stand with Mary your mother
and cry for the loss of your life.
And may I also stand
with the mothers of Michael Donald and Troy Davis,
George Floyd and Brionna Taylor,
Daunte Wright and Trayvon Martin,
and all the others who have lost their lives to injustice.
May I know their names.
May I honor their memory
by working for a safer world for all people of color.

—Patrick Saint-Jean, SJ
The Spiritual Work of Racial Justice

Help me, Spirit, to learn and hold in my heart
the names of all individuals killed by racism.
May I mourn them and work to build a safer world.

MARCH 20

SAINT CUTHBERT'S DAY

BRIDGE BUILDING

Faithful Cuthbert,
help us to resist the temptation to argue.
Instead, teach us to build bridges.
Wash from our hearts
the scorn, the frustration, and the contempt
that lead only to wider cracks
in our human community.
Give us strength and wisdom
to be more like you, a warrior for reconciliation.

—Meg Llewellyn
The Celtic Wheel of the Year

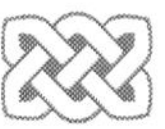

During the seventh century, Cuthbert worked
to build bridges of understanding.
In our polarized world, may we follow his example.

MARCH 21

SPRING EQUINOX

EQUILIBRIUM

Divine Creator,
you made the universe to work in perfect balance,
to find equilibrium in its natural rhythm and in you.
May my life reflect that balance.
I bring before you now
all that is within my life that brings imbalance.
As the Earth cycles,
and the balance of the light and dark are equal,
draw me to a place of equilibrium in you.

—David Cole
Celtic Prayers & Practices

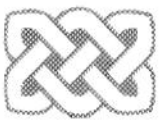

Show me, Lover-of-All-That-Is,
where in my life there is too much of something,
where there is too little, and how I can find balance.

MARCH 22

NEW LIFE

May we today, at the dawn of new life,
bless the Earth.
Teach us, O Creator God, to enrich the soil,
to put back what we have taken.
We depend on Your hand for our sustenance,
but we also depend on Your Earth for our sustenance.
The seed is in the Earth's belly,
and You have planted new life in our hearts.
We give You thanks
and ask that You bless the Earth,
bless human hands that work the Earth,
and bless the life You give.

—Meg Llewellyn
The Celtic Wheel of the Year

In this season of growing life,
may I seek to bless all of your Creation.

MARCH 23

GOD IS THE ONE

Why don't You answer me, Beloved God,
when I pray?
Why do I get nowhere in my spiritual life?
Why don't You help me?
And then Your answer comes to me:
"I was the One who called your heart to prayer.
I was the One who made you long for Me.
Your longing was My message to you.
Your voice calling out, 'God, God, God!'
was Me saying, 'Here I am.'
All your frustration, your sense of helplessness,
your yearning for something more,
all that was My voice speaking to you.
I was the magnet for your prayers,
and I am the One who made them fly."

—Rumi

Love Prayers

Teach me, Beloved, to sense your Presence
in my yearning and loneliness.

MARCH 24

A SINGLE WORD

You have drawn my love to you, Holy One.
I was asleep in my bedroom,
and Your voice woke me.
I was drowning in the deeps of the world's ocean,
and You saved me,
holding me in Your arms, O Holy One.
Only a single word—and you freed me
from all that bound me.
You have united my heart with Yours.

—Kabîr

You're Already Home

Wake me up, Holy One,
and make me one with you.

MARCH 25

NEW PATHWAYS

We need to create pathways that join faith and action
with the insights of the great wisdom traditions.
We grow in spiritual stature
by embracing rather than excluding.
We need to nurture great thoughts and expansive experiences,
and this comes from digging deep
into our own tradition's spiritual resources
as we also welcome the insights of other religious traditions.
This isn't a matter of personal preference but an affirmation
of the interdependence of life
and the universality of divine revelation.
We are both one and many
in the intricate interrelatedness of life.

—Bruce Epperly
Become Fire!

Instead of being threatened by other
beliefs, Spirit of Truth,
may I be willing to learn.

MARCH 26

A SEEKER

A seeker is someone who is satisfied
with neither her consciousness state
nor the accepted explanations of Reality.
A seeker courses beyond the surface chit-chat of human society,
beyond the dogma and doctrine of nationalism,
of corporatism, and other forms of religion.
A seeker finds that the outer infinity
and the inner infinity are the same infinity.
The seeker is disturbed . . . and then astonished
by finding Who is seeking.
All cognitive frames fall away and the seeker is silent,
in the silence out of which all arises.

—George Breed
The Hidden Words of Jesus

May I never stop seeking you, Spirit of Life.

MARCH 27

GOD'S SONG

I am the amoeba swimming in pond water.
I am the elephant stepping gently on huge feet.
I am the whale that sings its song seven fathoms deep.
I am the chickadee with dark bright eye.
I am the hawk rising swift on currents of wind.
I am the tiger stalking its prey.
I am the platypus, most confused of all animals.
I am the wild goose flying on strong winds.
I am the rabbit, fleet of foot and timid of heart.
I am the minnow, darting in shallow water;
the tadpole transforming into something new;
the caterpillar never dreaming of wings;
the butterfly that speaks to you of resurrection;
the cat curled in your lap; the spider spinning her web;
the cow, patient servant of humanity;
and the cricket, singing its autumn song.
I am the breath of each one. I am the Spirit in each.
I am everywhere you turn, if you only had eyes to see.

—Kenneth McIntosh
Celtic Nature Prayers

Spirit, give me eyes to see you everywhere.

MARCH 28

PAIN AND EGO

When we are in pain, we may be tempted
to summon moral indignation in our defense,
using it to isolate evil as a quality only in others,
rather than facing its reality in ourselves.
When we take that route, suffering can become
a means of consolidating our ego identity.
It can be something we wrap ourselves up in,
something we use as a shield—or wield as a weapon.

—Marc Thomas Shaw
Dante's Road

Show me, Spirit of Love, if I am using my pain
to support my identity, either as a shield or as a weapon.

MARCH 29

PRAYER FOR A WOUNDED EARTH

God who is Three-in-One, we know you see the sparrow fall.
Surely, you see each polar bear that dies
as Earth's polar ice melts.
Christ who is the Lamb slain, surely
you feel the pain of dolphins,
rhinos, gorillas, whales, and turtles,
dying from the wounds we have dealt your world.
God who is Mercy, forgive us for our sins against your world.
Give us eyes to see that as we wounded the Earth,
we have wounded you with our greed and ignorance.
Give us strength to change.
Bless each beast, bird, and fish, each plant and tree,
each insect and microbe, and each human
within your web of life.

—Ellyn Sanna
Celtic Prayers for Times of Crisis

Heal our wounds, Spirit of Life—
the wounds we have dealt the Earth,
the wounds we have dealt each other,
and the wounds we have dealt our own hearts.

MARCH 30

IN THE MIDST OF ORDINARY LIFE

We need the constant stream of God's Spirit.
That does not, however, necessarily mean
we must interrupt our daily routines for spiritual observances.
We can take delight in God
while going about our necessary tasks.
Celtic spirituality teaches us to celebrate God
in the everyday things of life.
To quote psychologist Carl Jung,
"Bidden or not bidden, God is present."
Infinite Compassion is always there,
irrigating our dry lives with its endless flood.

—Kenneth McIntosh
Water from an Ancient Well

Teach me, Spirit,
to drink from your waters all day long.

MARCH 31

GOD PRAYING IN US

We enter silence not to pray
but to have God pray in us.
We die to who we think we are.
We are not fathers, mothers, sisters, brothers, friends.
We are not our occupations,
the daily tasks that we perform, or our accomplishments.
We are not our to-do list. Nor are we our opinions,
our agenda, the sense of self-worth we feel
when we get a raise, receive a bonus,
or receive lavish praise and compliments from others.
We are not our feelings.
We enter silence to empty ourselves of all those things.
We enter silence to rest
in the arms of Infinite Love.

—Rich Lewis
Sitting with God

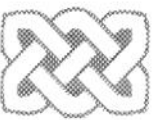

Remind me, Life-Giver, that my true identity
is found in your love.
Pray in me and through me today.

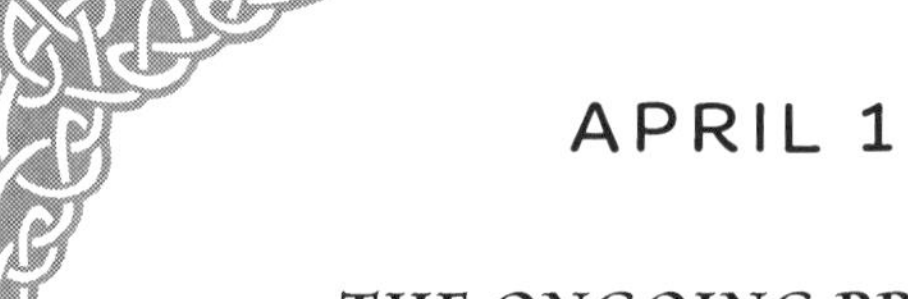

APRIL 1

THE ONGOING PROCESS OF CREATION

The Bible indicates that the Spirit of God
is in charge of both human conception
and the multiplication of ideas,
as in the original Creation.
This is a promise from the Creator
that things will evolve—
Creation is a continuing process—
and that stages of consciousness are involved
in the fulfillment of Divine Creation.

—Lynne Bundesen
The Feminine Spirit

Continue, Spirit, to move
through my inner and outer lives,
creating newness and expansion.

APRIL 2

THE LADDER OF LOVE

Stop looking for doctrines
and religious certainties.
You have no need of them,
for you are climbing life's ladder
that leads to the Beloved's door.
The only way you can find Love
is by loving.
Love is life. Love is creation.
Love is joy.
Love is the ladder that leads
to the Beloved's door.

—Hafiz
Love Prayers

Today, Beloved One, remind me
that as I love others, I draw nearer to you.

APRIL 3

DIVINE LIGHT

As the sun rises, and night wanes,
and then tonight, as another day comes to an end,
may I be fully aware, Ruler of the universe,
that never does the strength of your love wane from me.
As the Earth turns in its natural cycle
of day to night and night to day,
may I become aware of all within my inner world
that causes me to turn my back on you,
losing sight of your Divine Light.
May I know your presence
even when your Light seems to fade.
May I rest in the knowledge
that you, Life-Giver, will shine forever.

—David Cole
Celtic Prayers & Practices

May I never fear the changing cycles of life, Divine One,
for each one is lit by you.

APRIL 4

SPRING!

Renewing God,
spring has leapt into our midst:
may we spring into action with the same energy
to defend and save Your world.
Let Your seeds sprout in us,
so that we become restorers, defenders,
protectors of the planet.
Sweep away the cobwebs from our awareness,
and let the innate beauty
with which You dignified our souls
be profligate.

—Ray Simpson
Dance of Creation

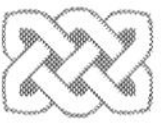

May today, Spirit, be a day of renewal
for my heart and mind.

APRIL 5

FOLLOWING JESUS

Jesus, I want to follow you, all the way to cross.
I want to be like Simon the Cyrene,
who did not let you carry your cross alone.
Show me how I can bring the power of the cross
into every situation of injustice and oppression I encounter.
I know I may stumble, just as you did on your way to Calvary,
but I know you are by my side, your hand outstretched
to help me get to my feet and continue on.
When the weight of racism overwhelms me, strengthen me.
When I'm tempted to despair, encourage me.
When I can no longer see the way, be my Light.
Jesus, I want to follow you.

—Patrick Saint-Jean, SJ
The Spiritual Work of Racial Justice

Help me to bring your light, Spirit of Love,
to racism wherever it exists,
both within me and in the world around me.

APRIL 6

A SINGLE LOVE SONG

Remind me, Loving One, that every person
has their own unique path to You,
and yet all paths are the same:
they all lead to You.
No matter what religion we follow—
or don't follow—
we all praise One Being.
May all our voices,
from our many ways of believing,
rise together, singing a single love song
to You.

—Rumi
Love Prayers

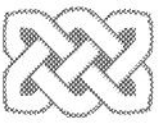

Teach me not to judge others
who see you differently than I do, Beloved.
Open my mind, so I can join the chorus of love.

APRIL 7

DIVINITY WITHIN OUR BODIES

God does not hold back from a single aspect of Creation,
nor does the Divine One disdain to serve us
in the simplest and most ordinary ways.
Think how neatly our food is contained within our bodies,
digested, and then is emptied out as needed,
like a lovely drawstring purse that opens and closes.
God is completely comfortable with all our bodies' activities;
none of them offend the Divine Presence,
for all our bodies' natural functions are Divine vehicles,
filled with the love God bears us,
whose souls are made in the Divine likeness.

—Julian of Norwich
All Shall Be Well

Thank you, Loving Spirit, that you
reject nothing about me.
Teach me to be just as comfortable
with each aspect of myself.

APRIL 8

EXPANDED VISION

We must widen our lens
in order to see beyond our barriers,
so that we can reach a deeper understanding
of the seeds of violence.
It's not enough to cry for justice and identify with the victim.
Growing toward wholeness means
also identifying with the pain of the victimizer.

—Marc Thomas Shaw
Dante's Road

Expand my vision, Spirit, so that I may see
beyond polarization, using your eyes of love.

APRIL 9

ATTENTION

Infants and young children notice everything.
As we grow, we pick up messages
(some spoken, some unspoken, some about survival itself)
about what we ought to focus on,
and most of us forget the scents and sounds of childhood,
such as the way the air smells just after it rains.
We get rewarded for "keeping our eyes on the prize,"
and we miss seeing the beauty of the roadside.
Remembering to notice and discerning what is actually vital
(as opposed to what I have been *told* is vital)
has been one of the spiritual practices of my life.

—Melina Rudman
Sacred Soil

Today, Spirit of Life, remind me to pay attention.
May this be my spiritual practice today and always.

APRIL 10

MOMENTS OF ETERNITY

We can experience eternity right here
in this very moment. We have these wonderful experiences
where we get a little taste, a little tease,
a little prologue of what eternity.
And these come through our senses.
Forever is right here. It is right now. It is in our body.
We experience this not in the desire
to escape this world and go to heaven
but by bringing a little bit of heaven to Earth.

—Jeff Campbell
Discovering the Essence

May I experience your timeless NOW, Spirit,
again and again throughout this day.

APRIL 11

DAILY WONDER

I invite you to tend the garden of social media
by posting positive messages and photographs.
Yes, there is good reason to challenge injustice and incivility,
and we are mandated to do so.
We are also mandated to share
out of our gratitude for the beauty of the Earth
and the amazing realities of life itself,
embodied in our daily lives of parenting, grandparenting,
sharing meals, reading books, and serving the community.
Celebrate daily wonders
in the course of your social media posting.

—Bruce Epperly
God Online

Let my words and meditations, my
posts and communications,
bring insight, healing, and beauty to the world.

APRIL 12

AN EVERYDAY GOD

Like traditional First Nations people,
the Celts perceived the interconnectedness of the universe.
So for the ancient Celts, God was not
just in holy places and high ceremonies;
Divine loving-kindness was
equally present in farmyards and on fishing boats.
They found it while they milked the
cows and washed their faces.
It spilled through every ordinary day.
The God described in the Bible is also an everyday God,
involved in the sweat and grime of life.

—Kenneth McIntosh
Water from an Ancient Well

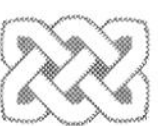

Teach me, Love-Bringer, to look for you
in the ordinary circumstances of each day.

APRIL 13

GOD BREATHING IN US

We enter silence, trusting in Infinite Love.
When we self-empty,
we allow the Holy Spirit to fill us.
We let the breath of God breathe within us.
We let God pray within our depths.
When we enter the spaces between our thoughts,
we experience God's Being.

—Rich Lewis
Sitting with God

Breathe in me today, Spirit.
May I experience you, both in silence and in busyness.

APRIL 14

A DEEPER JOURNEY

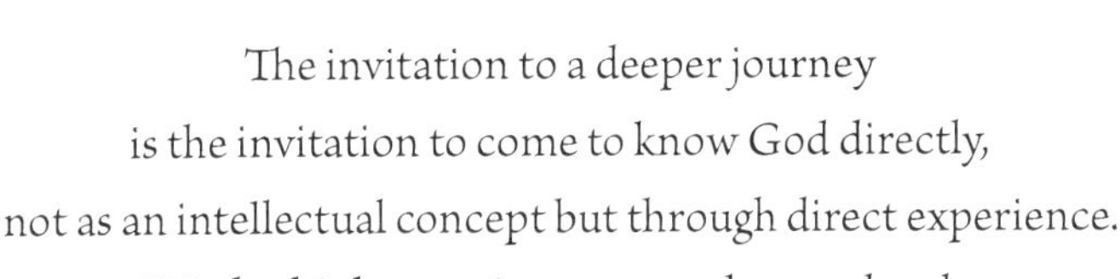

The invitation to a deeper journey
is the invitation to come to know God directly,
not as an intellectual concept but through direct experience.
We do this by moving more and more deeply
into our interior domain, into the well
where God dwells deep within us.
Many of us feel separated from God
because we have been looking for God
only beyond ourselves, as a separate Being.
We've been looking "out there," when all the while,
here God is, hidden in the depths of our own beings.

—Sharon Grussendorff
Deeper

Show me the way, Beloved One,
to find you within my own being.

APRIL 15

ON THIS DAY AND EVERY DAY

Loving Christ,
may I remember this day, and each day,
that You are the source of all mercies.
The warmth of sun, the bud, the seed,
all things swelling, the cow with calf,
the sheep with lamb, my heart with love,
all this You bestowed gently and generously.
This day and each day may I be fuller in love with You.
Each thing I have received, from You it came,
each thing for which I hope, from Your love it will come.
Each thing I enjoy is from Your bounty.
Each thing I ask comes in Your time.
Holy God, loving One, Word Everlasting,
lighten my understanding, kindle my will,
begin my doing, incite my love,
strengthen my weakness, enfold my desire,
on this day and every day.

—Meg Llewellyn
The Celtic Wheel of the Year

Fill me with your love today, Holy One.

APRIL 16

ENDLESS LIGHT

Beloved,
if I come to You because I fear Hell,
I don't deserve You.
If I seek You out because I long for Heaven,
I'll never find You.
"Spiritual" greed is no better than "worldly" greed.
Both revolve around my ego.
I need nothing in this world or the next,
only You.
Hell does not exist within Your presence.
Heaven is only You.
Give me, Beloved, the endless light
that streams from Your Face.

—Rabi'a
Love Prayers

Help me, Spirit of Love, to surrender my ego's desires,
so that I can come closer to you.

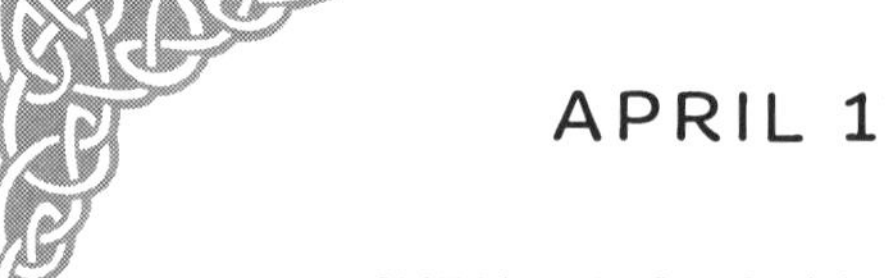

APRIL 17

SELF-UNDERSTANDING

When you understand yourselves,
says Jesus in the Gospel of Thomas,
then you will be understood. A reciprocity exists:
a process that happens naturally, automatically.
The more room I open within my being,
the greater room there is to be understood.
There is richness here, a new golden rule:
"Understand yourself as you would
have others understand you."
But the wealth of Jesus' statement
goes still deeper. We are embodyings of the Life Force,
of the energetic spirit of our Source.
As we begin to know that, to consciously embody
hat spirit, to awaken from any illusion of separation,
we create more room for the Life Force.

—George Breed
The Hidden Words of Jesus

Source of All Life, expand my self-understanding,
so that I have more room for you.

APRIL 18

HEALING DURING CLIMATE CHANGE

We pray, O Three-in-One,
for a world of rising temperatures, drought and flood,
wild weather and broken seasons,
failed crops and dying forests.
Creator God, in your mercy, renew this damaged world.
For each creature threatened by climate change,
we pray, O Three-in-One.
Creator God, in your mercy, renew this damaged world.
You who made the Earth, remake her now.
Give us love and strength to partner with you
and renew this damaged world.

—Ellyn Sanna
Celtic Prayer for Times of Crisis

Creator, show me how to help heal the Earth.
Help me to pray, to speak, to act.

APRIL 19

YES!

Power of the stars, sea, and sun,
empower me to join God's chorus of healing messengers.
Help me recognize the possibilities in life's limitations.
Give me insight to wisely bring light
and love to every encounter.
God of every tomorrow,
inspire me toward your new horizons of loving service.
Help me recognize and nurture your great "yes" in my life.
Help me nurture the Christ-Child being born in me.

—Bruce Epperly
From Cosmos to Cradle

Teach me, Spirit of Life, to make room
for the Divine Child to be born in my life.

APRIL 20

OUR INNER SHADOWS

We have to face our own shadows, our own shame,
our own fear, our own wounds.
This shadowy realm is the space that sets our boundaries;
it is the place where we live out much of our lives;
and yet it is also the space we avoid most,
the space we go to great lengths
to keep hidden from our friends and our families,
from our partners and even ourselves.
To find growth, to find maturity, to find our true homes,
we have to explore that space.

—Marc Thomas Shaw
Dante's Road

I ask, Spirit, for the strength I need
to face my inner shadows.

APRIL 21

COMING HOME TO OURSELVES

The inner journey involves being present
in our lives, in our bodies, in the present moment.
Spirituality is not some outer goal we strive toward
but rather a coming-home to ourselves:
learning to become present in our lives
and going deeper into who and where we are.
As we do this, we discover
an incredibly rich source of life and nourishment
the place where God resides within each of us.

—Sharon Grussendorff
Deeper

Help me recognize the place, Spirit,
where you reside in me.

APRIL 22

GOD'S VOICE

I began to see something I had never suspected:
God had been there, inside me, all along.
And if God was there—if God was my Self,
in some way I still didn't understand—
how could I hate myself the way I had
throughout my entire life?
All these years, had I been silencing *God's voice* within me?
This new thought gripped me with a terrifying joy,
a sense of amazed and incredulous awe.

—Marietta Bahri Della Penna
Song of a Christian Sufi

May I learn to hear your voice, Spirit of Love,
singing within my own Self.

APRIL 23

INTER-SPIRITUAL ADVENTURES

I believe that persons of other faiths
can learn from one another.
A robust commitment to your own religious tradition
can be the inspiration to seek wisdom
locally and globally, while remembering
that no image of the divine is ever complete.
As a Christian, fidelity to Christ
encourages me to commit myself
to interfaith and inter-spiritual adventures.
My understanding of the pathway of Jesus
is illuminated by my encounters with other faith traditions.

—Bruce Epperly
Become Fire!

May I always be willing, Spirit of Life,
to learn more about you,
even from unfamiliar sources outside my experience.

APRIL 24

DELIGHTING IN OUR BODIES

I am the beloved image of you, Life-Giver.
My body and face are gifts from you.
Help me to no longer listen to the lies
my culture whispers about my body.
Instead, may I delight
in the physical self you created for me.

—Kenneth McIntosh
Water from an Ancient Well

Remind me, Spirit, to take delight in my body,
no matter what its limitations may be.

APRIL 25

THE COMMITTED SEEKER

The committed seeker merges within her
the double currents of love and detachment,
like the mingling of two rivers.
In her heart, the sacred Water flows day and night,
and the cycle of birth and death comes to an end.
See! Wonderful rest is found in the Spirit;
the one who readies herself for it, relaxes there.
Held by cords of love, the swing of the Ocean of Joy
sways to and fro, and with a sound like thunder,
breaks into song.

—Kabîr
You're Already Home

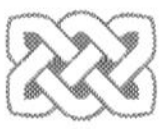

Help me, Spirit, to relax
in the swing and sway of your love.

APRIL 26

LIGHT AND DARKNESS

Science asserts that what humans discern as darkness
is actually filled with tiny slivers of light called "neutrinos."
Darkness is a falsehood and an illusion,
for no place is entirely dark.
John's account of his vision
recorded in the Book of Revelation—
the trumpet voice of Wisdom, the Glorious Cosmic Christ—
ends with a reminder that we carry Divine Light within us,
beacons of hope that the greatest darkness
cannot overcome.

—Kenneth McIntosh
Hope in an Age of Fear

Remind me, Light-Bringer, that darkness is not evil,
that darkness and light coexist,
and new life grows from darkness.

APRIL 27

CHRIST IN CREATURES

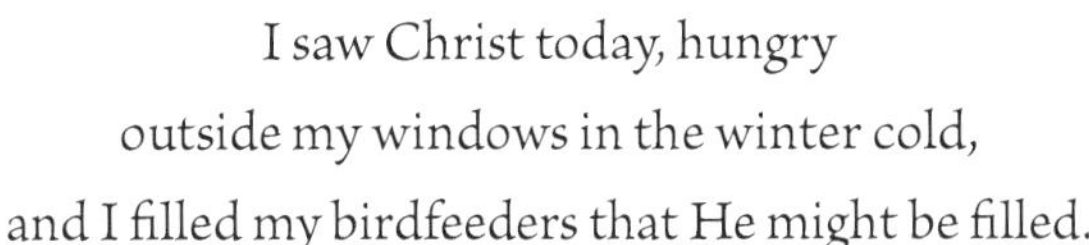

I saw Christ today, hungry
outside my windows in the winter cold,
and I filled my birdfeeders that He might be filled.
I saw Christ today,
running on swift hooves across the road,
and I slowed my car that He might be safe.
I saw Christ today, in the glad face of my dog,
as I greeted her at the end of the workday.
I saw Christ today,
in the moth that beat against the window,
until I let it out into the night.
Each time I saw Christ, He blessed me,
in the Holy Name of the Trinity,
and the bird outside my window sang again and again,
"Often and often, goes Christ on wing and hoof and paw."

—Ellyn Sanna
Celtic Nature Prayers

May I see you, Living One, present in all creatures.

APRIL 28

SILENT CONNECTION

In silence, we discover a connection with God
that is a deep-down profound affirmation
of the substance of our being.
We are hardwired for intimacy with
God, and when we find it, we naturally come
to embody a deeply rooted confidence,
stability, and positivity.
God waits for us in the silence, so we don't
need to fear it. In the depths of silence God
will speak to us.
Silence teaches us who we are.
We can trust the silence.

—Rich Lewis
Sitting with God

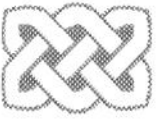

Help me, Spirit of Love, to trust the silence
where I can connect with both you and my true Self.

APRIL 29

SHEDDING OUR SKINS

We continue to shed the skin
of an enclosed consciousness
before it becomes a thick rind.
We do so by continuing to allow ourselves to be open,
to urge our established, settled, static selves
to be receptive to the newness of existing.
Our frozen rigidness falls away.
Soft, supple, with eyes of wonder,
we are alive.

—George Breed
The Hidden Words of Jesus

Keep me open, Spirit,
so that I can shed the hard rind of unconsciousness.

APRIL 30

ROOTS

THIS moment is the depth dimension into God.
By sinking deeper into now,
by staying present and open to what IS
(whatever arises, even despair or fear),
this is how the taproot of my heart
sinks into the Fertile Ground of Being. Only this.
The grit and stones that interfere with my roots
are all the mental grasping and conjecturing I get trapped in—
the church of the poison mind where I worship so often.
The simple gesture of noticing and letting go,
resigning and returning is all it takes.
Slowly, quietly, and surely, my roots
sink deep, and life and growth grows from them.

—Sharon Grussendorff
Deeper

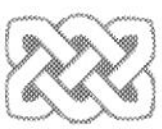

Ground of All Being, remind me to
stay rooted in the moment,
so that I can grow more deeply into your Spirit.

MAY 1

BELTANE

FIRE AND FLOWER

Bless, O Divine One, Queen of All,
on this day of fire and flower,
my family and myself, my pets, my plants,
all wild things that share my world,
and all children of the Great Mother.
Bless everything within my dwelling,
all my possessions, all my work.
I give them now to You, a crown of flame and flower.
On this May Day, bless everything and everyone I touch.
May Your tending follow them.
May Your blessing make them fruitful.
May Your love embrace them.
You who gave me birth, give birth now, I pray,
to Your work of fire and flower in each detail of my life.
Bless, O Divine One, Queen of Love,
on this day of fire and flower.

—Meg Llewellyn
The Celtic Wheel of the Year

Holy Mother, bless my life today
with the abundance of your life and joy.

MAY 2

OLD WOUNDS

Wrapping ourselves in the pain of our personal beginnings—
whether it stems from our culture, community, or family—
only breeds a sense of victimhood and possibly entitlement.
It can make us believe we are powerless
and can prevent us from growing.
Instead, as we look squarely at this suffering,
directing an unbroken gaze toward it,
we separate ourselves from it.
It is there, it is real, but it is not us.
Stepping back from the pain allows us
to find our true identities, while it expands
our ability for compassion and understanding.

—Marc Thomas Shaw
Dante's Road

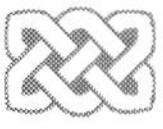

Spirit of Grace, give me the courage
to face the pain of old wounds,
even as I no longer let them shape my identity.

MAY 3

NEW VISIONS

Jesus, forgive me if I have ever worshipped
a false version of you.
I want to be open now to your full reality.
Give me the humility to seek you out
in the experiences and insights of people of color.
Show me where I am still clinging to any notions of superiority.
Help me be willing to learn new things
from those whose experiences have been different from mine.
Reveal yourself to me in new ways, I pray.

—Patrick Saint-Jean, SJ
The Spiritual Work of Racial Justice

Teach me, Spirit of Love, to be open to your teaching.

MAY 4

LEARNING FROM THE EARTH

You who put beam in moon and sun,
You who put fish in stream and sea,
You who put food in grain and herd,
send Your blessing up to us
through every blade and bud that pushes through the soil.
Bring forth the warmth, the tears, the laughter
from our repressed and frozen ground;
bring forth loving, healing, forgiving
to our fretting, festering wound.
May the Earth teach us what we need to know.
And may we be willing to learn.

—Ray Simpson
Dance of Creation

Creator, may your blessing be on this day,
and on the Earth that gives me life.

MAY 5

DANCING WITH THE DIVINE

When I was young,
I knew You, God, as all children do.
But not the God the grown-ups knew,
the God of don'ts
and big words I didn't understand.
The God I knew then
said only four words to me,
over and over:
"Come dance with Me!
Come dance with Me!"

—Hafiz
Love Prayers

Today, Beloved, if you see me weighed down
with anxiety and responsibilities,
remind me to DANCE!

MAY 6

CLOTHED IN GOD

Just as our bodies are clothed with fabrics,
our blood and muscles covered with skin;
our bones wrapped with blood and muscles,
and our hearts hidden at the center of all these—
so are we, soul and body, clad in the sweetness of God,
completely enclosed and safe.
Our clothing, our flesh, our very bones,
all may grow old and waste away—
but the sweetness and unity of God
are always whole and strong.
They are closer to us than our very bodies.

—Julian of Norwich
All Shall Be Well

Clothe me, Spirit, soul and body,
with your love, your life.

MAY 7

LIFE'S EVER-TURNING CYCLE

Life is a force that waxes and wanes, ebbs and flows.
All of life responds to the energy in all of life.
It affects and infects potted plants and human beings.
We may call it "spring fever," "summer love,"
"hibernation," or "seasonal affective disorder,"
but we are in it, and it is in us.
We are all subject to the seasons and the laws of life:
gestation, birth, life, aging, death.
What falls into the earth and dies
is reborn in the dark and emerges as new life.
What we grow in the shadows, produces fruit in the light.

—Melina Rudman

Sacred Soil

Spirit, may I learn the Earth's lessons,
surrendering to change, to death, and to new birth.

MAY 8

NOW AND NOT YET

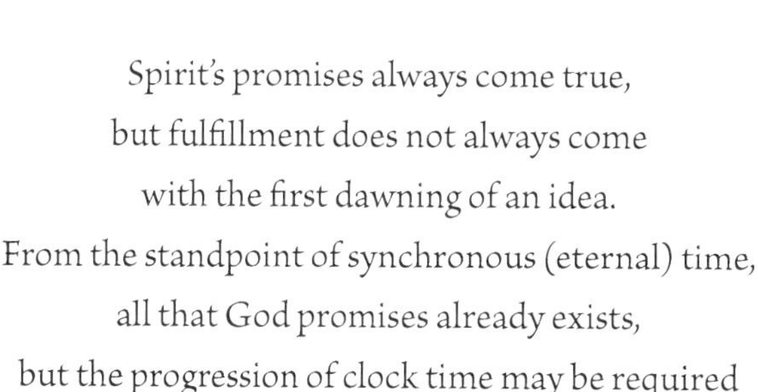

Spirit's promises always come true,
but fulfillment does not always come
with the first dawning of an idea.
From the standpoint of synchronous (eternal) time,
all that God promises already exists,
but the progression of clock time may be required
before we see the visible realization.

—Lynne Bundesen
The Feminine Spirit

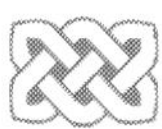

Teach me, Spirit, to live in hope and patience,
confident that your promises
are both "now" and "not yet."

MAY 9

THE PRESENCE OF GOD ONLINE

In practicing the presence of God
in our Internet interactions and in our postings,
we enable our own Divinity to burst forth,
as we discover ourselves to be God's messengers—
which is the literal meaning of angels—
of healing and reconciliation.
We create altars of healing and mindfulness
that transform our lives and contribute a sense of calm
to those around us.

—Bruce Epperly
God Online

Holy One, may my communications be in sync
with your Spirit moving through my
mind, heart, and fingers.
Let me be an instrument of peace.

MAY 10

THE FACE OF THE COSMOS

We humans generally move through the world
as if it were a mere backdrop
to our individual and societal melodramas:
Everything centers around Me and Mine.
In living this way, as inflated separate particles amid vastness,
we do not recognize what is right in front of us.
When we "come to" from our self-induced comas,
we begin to see what was hidden from us,
what we hid from ourselves.
The Face of the Cosmos is staring us in the face.
Nothing is hidden anymore,
for there is no place of separation for hiding.

—George Breed
The Hidden Words of Jesus

Bring me out of my spiritual coma, Living One,
so that I can see you.

MAY 11

THE EXAMPLE OF MARY

Mary of Nazareth was an unintentional activist.
She was a woman in a patriarchal society
and had little voice outside the confines of her household.
She was also of low estate, likely uneducated
and untrained in the ways of politics.
Yet the Gospel of Matthew envisions Mary
as a world-shaker and world-shaper.
She challenges the status quo
and invites us to also challenge injustice,
using our gifts to heal the spirit and economics
of our nation and the planet.

—Bruce Epperly
From Cosmos to Cradle

Thank you, Spirit, that you show me yourself
in the life of Mary of Nazareth.

MAY 12

THE BELOVED IS NEAR

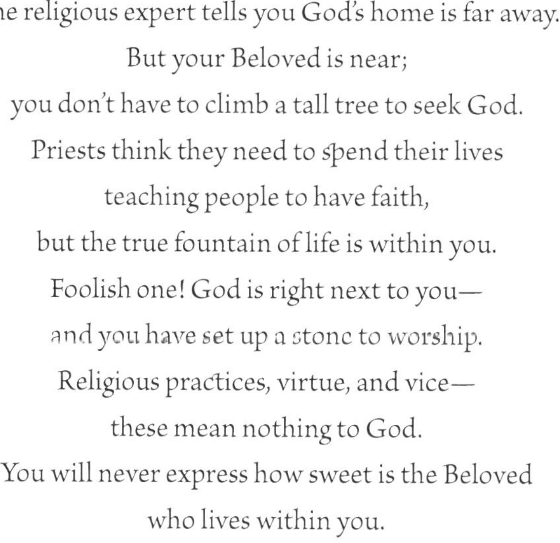

The religious expert tells you God's home is far away.
But your Beloved is near;
you don't have to climb a tall tree to seek God.
Priests think they need to spend their lives
teaching people to have faith,
but the true fountain of life is within you.
Foolish one! God is right next to you—
and you have set up a stone to worship.
Religious practices, virtue, and vice—
these mean nothing to God.
You will never express how sweet is the Beloved
who lives within you.

—Kabîr
You're Already Home

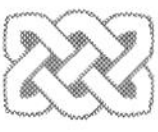

Teach me, Beloved,
to recognize you inside me.

MAY 13

PRAYER TO THE EARTH

Earth, teach me humility,
as blossoms are humble with beginning.
Earth, teach me courage, as the tree that stands alone.
Earth, teach me limitation,
as the ant that crawls on the ground.
Earth, teach me freedom, as the eagle that soars in the sky.
Earth, teach me regeneration,
as the seed that rises in the spring.
Earth, teach me to forget myself,
as melted snow forgets its life.
Earth, teach me hope,
as the bare trees wait for new leaves.

—Ellyn Sanna
Celtic Prayers for Times of Crisis

Give me the humility I need, Spirit of Love,
to learn from the Earth.

MAY 14

SECURE IN INFINITE MYSTERY

We both freefall into an infinite Mystery
and are upheld by God at the same time.
The deeper we fall, we never hit bottom,
for God has no limit.
We plunge into the depths of Mystery,
yet we are held securely by the love of God.
Faith is what allows us to take this leap into the unknown.
What do we have faith in?
That there is something much bigger than us.
We do not have to live in separation.
Instead, we can live in this Mystery;
we can participate in it, rest in it.
We are safe inside it, unconditionally loved.

—Rich Lewis
Sitting with God

Limitless God, I want to live in the Mystery that is you, knowing that I am secure, utterly and always.

MAY 15

FEAST OF SAINT DYMPHNA

TRAUMA AND HEALING

Dear One, young saint, courageous one,
you knew the pain of injustice, the violence of violation,
the loss of respect for boundaries,
and yet you remained true to yourself.
We ask your blessing now on all those who, like you,
are in danger of violation;
protect them and bring them justice.
We ask your blessing now
on all those who, like you, have been violated.
Restore them, we pray, and heal their hearts and flesh.
May they, like you, find that they still have
healing work to do, that their wounds
can make them strong enough to give to others who suffer too.
Dear One, young saint, may they, like you,
be blessed with courage, with determination,
and with healing love.

—Meg Llewellyn
The Celtic Wheel of the Year

Dymphna, a seventh-century Irish woman,
is the patron saint of victims of incest, teen runaways,
and those suffering from psychological problems.

MAY 16

SAINT BRENDAN'S DAY

VOYAGING BEYOND THE FAMILIAR

Help me to journey beyond the familiar
and into the unknown.
Give me the faith to leave old ways
and break fresh ground with You.
Christ of the Mysteries, I trust You
to be stronger than each storm within me.
I will trust in the darkness
and know that my times, even now, are in Your hand.
Tune my spirit to the music of heaven,
and somehow, make my obedience count for You.

—adapted from an ancient prayer credited to Brendan
The Celtic Wheel of the Year

In the fifth-century, Brendan set out on a sea voyage that may have taken him all the way across the Atlantic.

MAY 17

THIS DAY

Great Spirit of counsel, Almighty Three-in-One,
I give this day into your hands.
All that it is, all that it holds, and all that it will be,
I give it to you.
All the stresses and strains,
trials and tribulations that come my way,
I give them to you.
All the honour and worth,
praise and glory that would come my way,
I give them to you.
Keep my feet on the path you have set before me,
so that this day you ordained for me
before I was ever born will be fulfilled

—David Cole
Celtic Prayers & Practices

Spirit of Love, be a lamp to my feet
and a light to my path today.

MAY 18

GOD'S NUTRIENTS

Existence is a sacred place,
and no one lives outside its walls.
God is our Mother, whose eye is always on us.
Every time we cry,
Light reaches out Her arms.
The Beloved says to me,
"There is nothing you experience in this life
that will not lead you closer to Me.
You can go nowhere that will not nourish you.
Anything you encounter, I brought to you.
The world is full of My nutrients."

—Rabi'a

Love Prayers

Nourish me today, Mother God.

MAY 19

GATEWAYS TO GOD

If my body is a gateway to God,
then other bodies are as well.
And the whole of creation is.
Every single physical thing is God's artwork.
All of it bears the Divine signature.
All of it is an entryway into the transcendent.
If we can see God in anything,
we can begin to see God in everything.

—Jeff Campbell
The Divine Essence

Teach me, Living One, to see you in my own body,
in the bodies of others, in animals and plants,
and in the beauty of the world.

MAY 20

GOD MOMENTS

In the Celtic view of life,
all events take place in interaction with God.
We, the energies around us in the physical realm,
and the Divine Spirit all interact and co-create, constantly.
That means even the unpleasant happenings in our daily life
are potential opportunities to connect with God and others.
Consider commonplace annoyances,
like being stuck in traffic or waiting on hold—
what if you could turn those into "God moments"?
What if you took time
just to feel the air you are breathing in and out,
shifting your consciousness away from frustration
to a sense of awareness, opening yourself to the Spirit?

—Kenneth McIntosh
Water from an Ancient Well

Spirit, remind me today to turn to you
whenever I have opportunity.

MAY 21

MYSTERY

The faith journey will move us
from our entrenched collective ideas
into a much more personal, real space—
a space where we no longer only believe
what people have told us we should believe,
but where we find God in a place that's deeper
than the old answers can reach.
This is why, at some points in our spiritual journeys,
we may feel as though we are falling into an abyss.
This can be very frightening,
because this space is so much deeper
and more mysterious than our previous belief systems
can adequately explain.

—Sharon Grussendorff
Deeper

Give me the courage, Spirit,
to face the Mystery that is you.

MAY 22

HYMN TO THE PRESENCE OF GOD

Fiery Creator of fire, Giver of light, Life and Author of life,
I see You in fire, in light, in all of life.
I cannot see Your face, for I am blind,
wandering in the dark, yet You speak promises to me
in cloud, in starlight, in moon and sun.
You call out to me in morning light,
in light that ripples on water,
on candlelight that glimmers in darkness.
Though You are a consuming fire,
You do not burn what You illumine.
I taste Your sweetness in the recesses of the bee's comb.
The sweet food of Your honey
fills the inmost cells of my heart, and I am filled.
The bees swarm into the air; may, I like them,
win heaven on wings now free from care.

—Ellyn Sanna
Celtic Nature Prayers

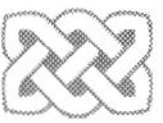

Today, Giver of Life, may I celebrate you
in the messages from my senses.

MAY 23

HEALING AND WHOLENESS

Everything God does is aimed at healing and wholeness,
beauty, and reconciliation. In quiet moments,
we can hear God's heartbeat, the heartbeat of love,
beating within our heartbeat and giving us energy
to become "healed healers," who share
what we have received.
God wants us to experience abundant life.
God wants creation in all its wondrous diversity
to bathe in an abundance of love, creativity,
respect, and possibility.

—Bruce Epperly
101 Soul Seeds for Healing and Wholeness

Holy One, Giver of Life and Love, let me experience your healing touch—and share it with all Creation.

MAY 24

CONFRONTING OUR SHADOWS

Our own personal shadows
contribute to the world's pain,
but the shadow's effects are also intimate and ordinary:
when we explode in anger at our child,
our shadow has taken control;
if we feel a need to show off our luxury car
or constantly pepper our conversation
with our accomplishments, it's our shadow talking;
our never-ending judgment of others
comes from our shadow, and it's at the root
of the falsehoods we tell to make ourselves seem more loveable.
To move toward wholeness,
we have to confront that aspect within ourselves.

—Marc Thomas Shaw
Dante's Road

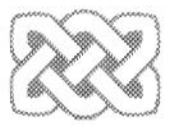

Teach me, Spirit of Wisdom,
to recognize when my shadow-self is controlling my life.

MAY 25

MANY SIDES

The Jains, followers of a spiritual path
twenty-five hundred years old,
believe in *anenkantavada*—the many-sidedness of reality.
Its meaning is not so much that everyone is right,
no matter what they believe, but rather
that there are many truths about the same thing.
In a polarized, take-no-prisoners political climate,
we would all do well to remember "many-sidedness,"
rather than insist on our own individual beliefs.
Doing so empowers us to hold fast to the pure love
that all faith traditions affirm.

—Kenneth McIntosh
Hope in an Age of Fear

May I always remember, Spirit of Love,
that you care more about love than "being right."

MAY 26

DIRT

In the physical world, humus is good soil.
In the spiritual realm, humus translates
into "humble," into "humility."
To receive increased understanding,
we must become the dirt we are.
Surrender is a word we all detest
yet surrender is exactly what is needed.

—George Breed
The Hidden Words of Jesus

Remind me, Giver of Life, that "surrender" and "humility" root me in the deepest spiritual soil.

MAY 27

MOTHER MARY

Mary of Nazareth, mother of Jesus,
whose love makes way for Divine revelation,
enlighten our path and guide our ways
that we might go from self-interest to world loyalty.
Let us be mothers and midwives
of Holy Adventure and New Creation,
life-givers in a world enamored of death.
Fill us with the Divine Energy that makes seedlings sprout
from the ashes of destruction.

—Bruce Epperly
From Cradle to Cosmos

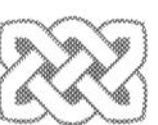

Spirit of Love, help me to be like Mary,
who gave birth to Love.

MAY 28

THE GREAT FAMILY

Together, we pray for all Creation.
Together, we love all God's creation.
Together we feel the love of a great family
reaching back generations and forward to generations unborn.
This extended family includes all our relations,
who share our DNA, and it also includes four-leggeds,
creepy-crawlies, and mountain ferns,
and even the trace metals from stars
that course through our circulatory system.
Divine love is in every tiny atom of Creation.

—Rich Lewis
Sitting with God

Thank you, Life-Giver, that I belong to such a vast family. May I play my part today in your work of love.

MAY 29

BLESSING

To bless means to confer goodness and abundance.
It is to acknowledge the sacredness of the thing which we bless,
To affirm God's ability to work through it in ways that bring life
(as when we "ask the blessing" on our food).
During times of crisis, we are called to do more than endure;
we are called to actively bless the people
and circumstances around us.
In doing so, we open up events to the Divine hand.
We not only allow God room to work, however,
but we also become actively part of the process.
In blessing others, we too are blessed
creating a chain strong enough to lead us through this crisis.

—Ellyn Sanna
Celtic Prayers for Times of Crisis

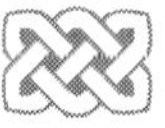

May I bring blessing, Spirit of Love,
to each person and situation I encounter today.

MAY 30

WATER IN THE WILDERNESS

In the story of Hagar and Ishmael,
Spirit is vocally present,
as She is with other seemingly powerless
and rejected biblical women.
As Hagar and her child, cast out and denied
by those who should have cared for them,
are thirsting to death in the wilderness,
God opens Hagar's eyes, and she sees
what was apparently there all along—a well of water.
The Divine Spirit, who once moved
on the face of the waters for the entire Cosmos,
now moves in a specific, life-saving way
for Hagar and her child.

—Lynne Bundesen
The Feminine Spirit

When I feel alone and rejected, Spirit,
reveal to me your living water.

MAY 31

THE TREE OF LIFE

Many ancient cultures have revered
the symbol of the Tree of Life;
my favorite image of this is a tree enclosed within a circle,
its branches and roots perfect mirrors of each other:
one above ground and visible,
the other below ground and hidden.
"As above, so below. As within, so without."
We are each a tree of life.
We live upon a small, blue and green planet
within a thin and fragile atmospheric bubble.
Our branches are interwoven.

—Melina Rudman
Sacred Soil

May I be rooted in the soil of your love, Life-Giver,
so that my branches bear fruit that will nourish others.

JUNE 1

SACRED TIME

The modern Western world thinks of time as a commodity,
something that can be measured,
as though it were a tangible substance.
Time is literally worth money, since most of us are paid
either by the year or the hour.
We also often begrudge time as a thief
that's determined to rob us.
For many indigenous cultures, however,
including the ancient Celts, time itself was sacred,
a way to connect and reconnect with
a larger spiritual awareness.
From this perspective, even going to bed at night
becomes an act of worship.
We may not be able to totally transform our linear,
commodity-based time consciousness—
but we can nevertheless
learn a richer, deeper way of looking at time, one that recognizes
the Divine Presence in the passing of each moment.

—Kenneth McIntosh
Water from an Ancient Well

May I see in the passage of time, Life-Giver,
new depths to explore with you.

JUNE 2

THE DIVINE LOVER

You are a creative Lover
with many positions for loving,
ten thousand different ways to embrace me:
each curve of a tree branch, the world's infinite shapes,
spring's orchestra of scents, the daily explosion of light,
all are like passionate lips against my skin.
Existence twirls her skirt,
countless universes hidden in the folds.
You feel my every breath,
falling against Your inconceivable,
everywhere-present
Body.

—Hafiz
Love Prayers

May I enter into a passionate love relationship
with you, Lover of my soul.

JUNE 3

MY NEIGHBOR

When you see me closing my eyes, Jesus,
unwilling to see the pain of my neighbor,
remind me of what you said about the Good Samaritan.
Make me willing to look,
to go out of my way, to spend my resources,
to do anything I can to help.
I know I can't pretend I love you,
unless I'm willing to give myself away in love
to my neighbor, whomever she is,
whatever he looks like,
wherever they lie bleeding.

—Patrick Saint-Jean, SJ
The Spiritual Work of Racial Justice

Open my eyes, Spirit, to those who
are in pain around me.
Help me to give myself in love.

JUNE 4

THE ENERGY OF GOD

God of the rising green,
God of the sweeping blue,
God of the long bright day,
may we, too, give glory to You.
God, eternally awake,
may Your energies flow through us.
God of the rising sap,
may we be Your sap today,
flowing through the Earth,
carrying Your green, life-giving energy
to all that is.

—Ray Simpson
The Dance of Creation

Fill me with your energy, Divine One.

JUNE 5

LOVING EVERYONE

I seek You, Beloved,
by loving everyone I meet.
Help me to see only good in them.
May I lift them up
when they are with me
and never pull them down
behind their backs.
Make me like a morning breeze,
sweet and warm.
Make me like the sun,
shining warmth on everyone.

—Abu Sa'id Ibn Ab'il Khair
Love Prayers

Remind me today, Beloved, to spread love.

JUNE 6

CLINGING TO GOD

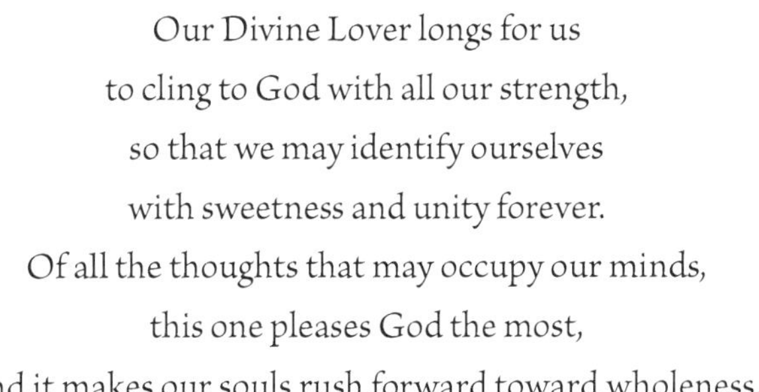

Our Divine Lover longs for us
to cling to God with all our strength,
so that we may identify ourselves
with sweetness and unity forever.
Of all the thoughts that may occupy our minds,
this one pleases God the most,
and it makes our souls rush forward toward wholeness.

—Julian of Norwich
All Shall Be Well

I cling to you, Beloved One,
and in you I become whole.

JUNE 7

EMBODIED SPIRITUALITY

A healthy sense of embodiment and mindfulness,
can make many things feel magical
that once seemed quite "secular"
or "profane" or "nonspiritual"
We can approach difficult conversations,
washing the dishes, mowing the lawn, making love,
even paying the bills, as spiritual practices.

—Jeff Campbell
Discovering the Essence

Today, God of Life, may each thing I do
be a spiritual practice that leads me
into a greater awareness of you.

JUNE 8

SEEDS OF PROMISE

"In your seed," God promises Abraham in Genesis,
"all the nations shall be blessed";
as in the Creation, the seed is within itself,
carrying a promise that reaches far beyond
the chronological time of Abraham and Sarah,
into cosmic, synchronous time.
Promises that are seeds and seeds that are promises.
Fulfilled promises, both in chronological and cosmic time.
New birth, both of flesh and spirt.
Nothing is impossible to Spirit. Creation is revealed
to complex human consciousness, regardless of gender.
That's the story of Sarah, Hagar, and Abraham.
It is a story that lives today.

—Lynne Bundesen
The Feminine Spirit

Plant your seeds in my life, Spirit;
carry out your endless creation in me.

JUNE 9

FEAST OF SAINT COLUMBA

REJOICING

By the singing of hymns eagerly ringing out,
by thousands of angels rejoicing in holy dances,
and by the four living creatures full of eyes,
with the twenty-four elders
casting their crowns under the feet of the Lamb of God,
the Trinity is praised in eternal threefold exchanges.

—Saint Columba
The Celtic Book of Days

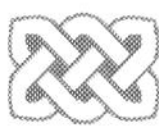

Spirit of Joy, may I, like Columba in the sixth century,
join the eternal song of joy that never ends.

JUNE 10

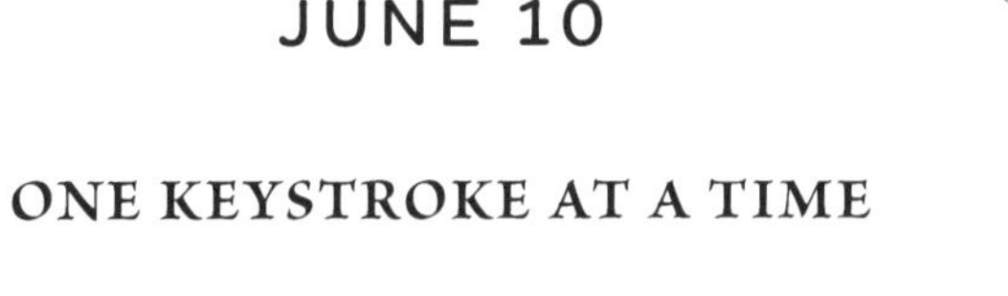

ONE KEYSTROKE AT A TIME

My spiritual counsel
to my social media companions is this:
When you find yourself upset at a post,
pause to consider—
What's pushing my buttons here?
Why do I need to be right in this situation?
What would it be like to be a Mahatma or Little Christ,
big-spirited enough to embrace diversity
without losing my spiritual centeredness?

—Bruce Epperly
God Online

Bless my thoughts as I communicate
and my fingers as I type that I might bring beauty, truth,
goodness, and holiness into the world, playing my part
in healing the world one keystroke at a time.

JUNE 11

ANGER

It is okay to get angry at God.
In fact, it makes perfect sense at times,
given the state of our world.
Being real with God about our feelings is a sign of intimacy.
When it comes to our relationship with God,
any and all feelings are acceptable;
all were known to Christ.
The real killer of intimacy is not volatile emotions
but indifference.

—Rich Lewis
Sitting with God

Thank you, Sprit, that you accept
and welcome all my emotions.
Teach me to bring my anger, my despair,
and my boredom to you (as well as my joy).

JUNE 12

THE DEATH OF THE FALSE SELF

One of our deepest fears is that
to give up our ego's programs for happiness,
to give up what the False Self seeks, is to give in to death.
At the most basic level, we fear death
because we believe we are this body,
we are these thoughts, we are these emotions.
In fact, we have all these things,
and we need to be good stewards of them,
but over-identifying with them keeps us caught in the False Self.
It takes a death—a true death,
in the healthiest sense of that word—
to free us from that illusion and open us
to the deeper sea of grace, both for ourselves
and for others.

—Marc Thomas Shaw
Dante's Road

Spirit, give me the energy, the commitment,
and the courage to let my False Self die.

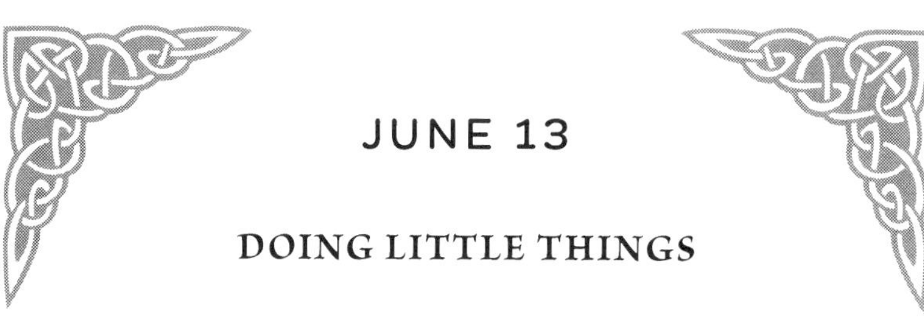

JUNE 13

DOING LITTLE THINGS

Clearly, we don't have to leave our jobs or families
and join a monastery in order to be immersed in the sacred.
Doing the little things—observing sacred
days, saying brief prayers
throughout the day, lighting a candle, inhaling incense,
or touching a reminder with our fingertips—
can create a canal system of life-giving spiritual water.
Without it, our souls may become arid and barren.

—Kenneth McIntosh
Water from an Ancient Well

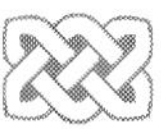

Show me, Beloved One, ways I can
weave reminders of you
through my daily routine.

JUNE 14

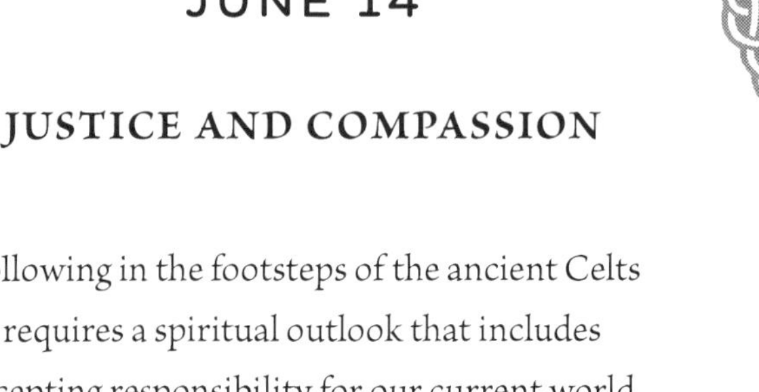

JUSTICE AND COMPASSION

Following in the footsteps of the ancient Celts
requires a spiritual outlook that includes
accepting responsibility for our current world.
It insists that we cannot be faithful to God
if we are not faithful to our entire community
(a community that not only includes
humans, but also animals, plants, and the entire Earth).
It is a mystical experience of the Divine
that expresses itself in acts of tangible justice
and compassion.

—Ellyn Sanna
Persistent Resistance

Show me, Just One, your path of compassion.

JUNE 15

HEALING LOVE

Healing is many-faceted and embraces the whole of life.
Nothing is off-limits for God's healing love.
No one is outside God's vision of wholeness.
Sin and sickness, and division and disease,
are never the final word. The final word is Love,
the Love that creates the Universe, guides the galaxies,
inspires the imagination, and awakens us
to healing waters in Creation with all its
wondrous, sometimes chaotic and confused,
and always evolving wonder and beauty.

—Bruce Epperly
101 Soul Seeds for Healing and Wholeness

Spirit, empower me be a catalyst for
creative transformation.

JUNE 16

LIMINAL SPACES

The Latin word for threshold is *limina,*
the space where you are not in one room
or the other but in between both.
Metaphorically, liminal spaces are encountered
as we outgrow old beliefs and habits
but have not yet fully entered into new ones.
These are places of possibilities
but places we cannot linger in for long.

—Melina Rudman
Sacred Soil

Teach me, Spirit, to recognize the liminal spaces
in my life—and meet you there.

JUNE 17

LOVED

Sufism acknowledges one central truth:
that we are not separate from the Divine,
nor have we ever been. And yet at the same time,
we know that the Beloved is always the initiator:
God loves us long before we love Him,
He is pursuing us before we ever think to pursue Him.
But we can recognize this only by unveiling our inner eye,
that is, the eye of the heart, and seeing
what we have not perceived before.
Until this happens, we walk around blinded,
mistaking what we see as reality.
The life we build when we are in this state
is nothing but a bed of straw.

—Marietta Bahri Della Penna
Song of a Christian Sufi

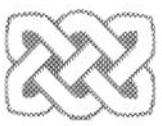

Beloved, I rejoice in our union of love.

JUNE 18

SACRED SPACE

Nature is a doorway into the other-than-human world,
which is more than plants and animals.
It reveals secrets about its Creator and it's somewhere
God can speak to us; Nature is sacred space.
Worship and ritual have become synonymous
with the inside spaces of temples and churches—
but in enclosing our spiritual practices,
we have separated ourselves from one of the greatest,
most vibrant sources of Divine revelation.

—Bruce Stanley
Forest Church

May I see you, Creator, in Nature's sacred spaces.

JUNE 19

JUNETEENTH

MOURNING AND CELEBRATION

America's work of mourning requires, I believe,
that we participate in *Sankofa*: returning to the past
in order to heal the present.
Then, as we confront the reality of racism and death,
we will also find rich potential and hope,
for in the Black experience lie answers
to our current fears and failures.
The Black experience is essential to our shared identity.
When we realize that, we will finally be able
to reclaim our kinship as blood sisters and brothers,
members of the same ancient family.

—Patrick Saint-Jean, SJ
Home-Going

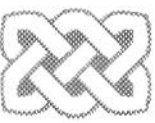

Thank you, Father of us all, for the human family,
with all its richness and variety.

JUNE 20

FACING PAIN

When I stop running from my hurt
And spend a moment occupying that space,
I usually discover two things quite quickly.
The first thing I discover is that when I turn off
all my distractions, all my attempts to ignore my pain,
what I feel is not as bad as I thought it would be.
I suspect the energy I put into trying to shield myself
from this makes it worse, not better.
The second thing I discover is that
even if the suffering was intense, it is just suffering
It doesn't kill me to experience it.
I am reminded that I am not my suffering,
that this suffering is only an experience I am having.
I can watch my suffering with interested compassion,
and in doing that, I learn that I am so much more
than my suffering.

—Jeff Campbell
Discovering the Essence

Give me courage, God of Love, to face my pain.
Remind me that it does not define who I am.

JUNE 21

THE LONG LIGHT OF SUMMER

God of the long day,
You who are eternally awake,
Your energy flowing out like song,
I offer You my eternal yes,
the flower of my humanity
the energy and awareness of my days,
the creativity of my life,
the beauty of all Earth's forms,
and the hope of future potential.
God of the long day,
may our lives be long days lit by You,
always reflecting Your light,
open and awake.

—Ray Simpson
The Dance of Creation

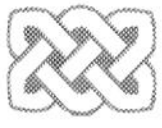

Shine your light into my life today, Creator.

JUNE 22

SUMMER SOLSTICE

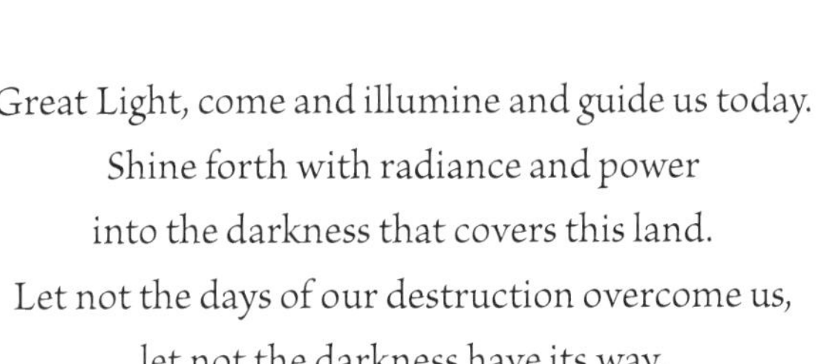

Great Light, come and illumine and guide us today.
Shine forth with radiance and power
into the darkness that covers this land.
Let not the days of our destruction overcome us,
let not the darkness have its way.
Leave us not to our own evil devices and any unkind way,
but come and shine with brilliance over this land.
Raise us again into that which we have been,
and can be again in you.
Light of the world, shine within me today.
Shine from within me today and all days henceforth.
Let naught but you be indwelling in me,
And naught but you stand out in me.
Great Light, be my guide and hold me fast,
that I may be the light upon a hill that cannot be hidden.
Shine forth from within me, now and ever more.

—David Cole
Celtic Prayers & Practices

May your light shine out from me today, Light-Giver.

JUNE 23

THE LATITUDES OF HEAVEN

Every line of all Your latitudes
circles the equator in my heart,
"Hello!" I shout to all my thousand forms.
I surf the invisible wave that flows from You
and carries me back home.
All of heaven's latitudes are sitting around a campfire
talking among themselves,
as they stitch themselves together
into the one Great Circle that is You,
the same Great Circle
that is in me.

—Hafiz
Love Prayers

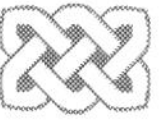

Today, Beloved, may I be more aware
that my life is part of your Great Circle.

JUNE 24

FEAST DAY OF JOHN THE BAPTIST

GRACE

Today is the day of grace,
the form of Christ before you, the form of God behind you,
the stream of the Spirit through you, to strengthen and aid you.
Grace upward over you, grace downward over you,
grace of graces that cannot be dammed.
Grace of Creator, grace of Son and Spirit,
grace of John of the Wilderness,
grace of sun, grace of light, grace of form and fortune,
grace of voice and word, grace of Jesus Christ be always yours,
grace of the image of God be yours.

—adapted from the *Carmina Gadelica*
The Celtic Wheel of the Year

Today is considered to be the birthdate
of John, the forerunner of Jesus,
who called for people to change their
course and follow the Son of Light.

JUNE 25

FREEDOM FROM EGO

Stilling yourself completely, you free yourself from your ego;
in New Testament terms, you "die to self."
In this quiet interior place, you are freed from judging others—
and from judging yourself. You are free from the voices that say,
"I must do . . . ," "I ought to . . . ," and "I should."
You are even free from "I am . . ."
When you are no longer aware of any "I,"
then you are able to enter fully into the presence of God
who resides within you; now it is no longer you who live
but Christ who lives in you (Galatians 2:20).

—Kenneth McIntosh
Water from an Ancient Well

Life-Giver, remind me to seek you today
in small moments of stillness.

JUNE 26

LIFE ITSELF

The Bible's Hebrew word *YWHW*
actually means "the Existing One,"
with additional inherent meanings having to do
with being, becoming, and becoming-like.
These enfolded implications show us a Divine One
who is not static but living and in motion,
the inclusive epitome of life itself.

—Lynne Bundesen
The Feminine Spirit

Open my eyes, Spirit, to your revelation
in the unfolding circumstances of life.

JUNE 27

ACTIVISM

The Celts were truly activists for justice.
They stood up for women and others
who were endangered by prejudice; and they worked
with tireless love on behalf of all of Earth's creatures.
They resisted the injustice of their day—
And they persisted throughout their entire lifetimes,
until their deaths. (And some would say that they are still
hard at work fighting injustice from the Otherworld.)
For the Celtic Christians, activism was not a sometime thing,
an activity to be engaged in now and then
when it was convenient. Instead, it was the constant,
lived expression of their connection to God, humans,
and the Earth. It was life itself.

—Ellyn Sanna
Persistent Resistance

May my relationship with you, Spirit,
express itself in the work of justice.

JUNE 28

THE SECOND BOOK OF GOD

Nature could be described as the Second Book of God.
Some may argue that it's the first book of God.
Whichever way, I do recognize the importance
And authority of the sacred scriptures,
but I don't think they're the only revelation about God
and I don't think Jesus thought so either.

—Bruce Stanley
Forest Church

Today, Spirit of Life, may I read your truth
in the natural world around me.

JUNE 29

THE DEAD AND THE LIVING

While living only to satisfy the body, we are spiritually dead.
When we do not live in accord with the Flow of the Life Force
that is forever birthing us, we are dead
to the energy of the Cosmos.
We feel a sense of separation that puffs and snorts
with disconsolate emotion and false inflation.
Those who recognize their identity with this eternal birthing,
however, never die. They are the embodying
of the Life Force, of the out-breathing
of the Spirit that never dies.
The deep awareness of this is the second and true birth.

—George Breed
The Hidden Words of Jesus

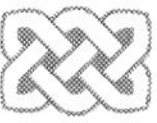

Birther of All Life, may I be aware today
that your Force breathes in me.

JUNE 30

LISTENING TO GOD

If I had a friend who only talked to me
and never took the time to listen, I would feel hurt.
I too want to be heard.
A healthy relationship involves both—speaking and listening.
To listen is to open a space for another
and let them fill it.
God speaks to us every day.
It is we who choose not to notice.
Silence is how we listen to God.

—Rich Lewis
Sitting with God

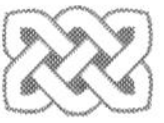

Spirit of Love, remind me to listen for your messages,
interwoven throughout my everyday life.

JULY 1

WAITING

In our busy society, where "time is money,"
waiting is to be avoided.
Before the Industrial Revolution, though,
When most of us still sang in unison with the land we tended
and depended upon, waiting was as important as action.
Plant too soon, and you might lose your crop to frost.
Harvest too soon, and your grain and fruit
would be unfit for consumption.
Human beings learned to wait,
and to fill their waiting with meaning.

—Melina Rudman
Sacred Soil

Teach me, Spirit, to wait patiently,
content in each moment, for you are always present.

JULY 2

JESUS' VOICE

Give me ears to hear your voice, Jesus.
May I be willing to hear you calling to me
as I listen to people of color.
Show me when I am being defensive
or unwilling to step free of my attachments and assumptions.
Bring me ever closer to you,
so that together we can work to build the Reign of Heaven.

—Patrick Saint-Jean, SJ
The Spiritual Work of Racial Justice

Point out any prejudice in me, Life-Giver,
anything that keeps me from being
an open and active conduit of your love.

JULY 3

WE GO FORTH

We go forward in the light of sun,
in the strength of earth, in the flow of water.
We go forth with the desert hermits
and the holy martyrs,
with all the holy and risen ones.
We go forth with the word of the apostles
and the wisdom of the seers,
with the angels above,
and the prayers of all God's people.
We go forth with each creature,
each tree, each blade of grass;
together, we sing Your song.

—Ray Simpson
The Dance of Creation

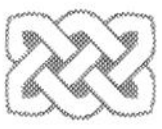

May your song, Living One,
be the background of my life today.

JULY 4

TRUE INDEPENDENCE

Not long ago, as I was helping a good friend of mine
process her grief after the death of a child,
she said something I had never articulated before:
"Death is the way we come to realize our new self.
It's a chance for reinvention, rebirth.
It offers regeneration that helps us survive
when surviving is impossible." And maybe that's exactly it:
death makes the survival of the old life impossible.
If we want to continue to live,
we must let the old way of being die—
so that something new can be born.
This, I believe, is also the challenge America faces.

—Patrick Saint-Jean, SJ
Home-Going

Help us, Spirit of Life, to die to old ways,
so that we can come to life anew, growing
into the people and societies you call us to be.

JULY 5

MORE ROOM FOR LOVE

If I could recite from memory a thousand scripture verses,
that wouldn't erase my ego-self.
Knowledge of scripture doesn't prove my worth,
when my ego-love proclaims my heresy.
Each time I bow in prayer, remind me, Beloved,
to drop the load of ego I carry on my back.
My ego is the bulky thing that makes me too fat
to get through the door into Your bedroom.
Feed my mind with tolerance, Beloved, and with compassion.
Simplify my life, so there's more room in it for love.

—Abu Sa'id Ibn Ab'il Khair
Love Prayers

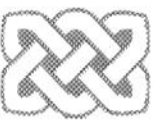

Help me, Spirit of Love,
to nudge my ego out of the way,
so that you can enter me—and I can enter you.

JULY 6

TRUSTING YOURSELF

Trust your own intuition.
Somewhere along your spiritual journey,
you might find yourself struggling
to trust your own voice.
This is a sad, sad thing.
More than anything else,
I hope, dear friend, that you feel confident
in knowing what you know, loving what you love,
trusting in the things
you think you want for yourself.

—Jeff Campbell
Discovering the Essence

Spirit who lives within me, help me today to trust myself. When I trust myself, I'm also trusting you.

JULY 7

THE STAIRWAY FROM EARTH TO HEAVEN

One interpretation of Jacob's vision
sees it as a reflection of cosmic, spiritual time,
revealing a living and dynamic unity between the genders.
In the Hebrew language "earth" is feminine,
and "sky" or "heaven" is masculine,
and here we have an image of a stairway
that connects the two, allowing God's messengers
to go back and forth between them.
The men and women in Jacob's family
have made a royal mess of things,
just as Eve and Adam did, but once again,
God promises to heal and restore.
Creation is unending.

—Lynne Bundesen
The Feminine Spirit

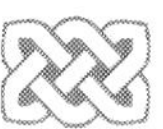

Show me, Spirit, the "stairways"
that connect the polarizations in my life.

JULY 8

LONGING FOR GOD

Our souls are so beloved of the Highest One
that we cannot completely comprehend
how tenderly our Maker loves us.
That is why, in grace and with Divine help,
we can stand up straight as we use our spiritual vision,
overwhelmed with endless awe
for the boundless, immeasurable love God shows us.
And that is why we may humbly ask our Divine Lover
for whatever we want.
For our natural and innate desire is for God—
and God's desire is for us.
Our longing will never end till at last,
in complete and utter joy, we possess God's fullness.
Then all our desires will be met.

—Julian of Norwich
All Shall Be Well

Thank you, Beloved, that in you,
all my desires are satisfied.

JULY 9

PROTECTED BY DIVINE LIGHT

Recognizing that we are surrounded by God's protection
and that nothing can separate us from the love of God,
we discover that others' posts can't threaten us,
nor do they need to ensnare us in controversy.
God's armor of light surrounds us and illumines us
as we navigate the minefields
of social media communication.

—Bruce Epperly
God Online

Guide me to the path of wholeness of love, Life-Giver,
that my social media conversations
might become sanctuaries of grace,
motivated by your ongoing quest
for wholeness and healing.

JULY 10

THE WORK OF JUSTICE

I cannot profess to work for justice
if I am occupied by anything but love—
the practical, muscular love that is up-close,
responsive, and immediate. This sort of love
is not easy, nor does it come naturally
to my ego-driven tendencies.
Nevertheless, that is the real meaning of justice,
and I cannot be my true self—wearing my true face—
unless I seek justice in all my interactions.

—Marjorie Bennett
Persistent Resistance

Spirit, may my life be guided
by the justice of your love.

JULY 11

BLESSING IN TIMES OF ANXIETY

When your soul cries out in fear,
may the God of peace quiet you.
When the world shakes beneath your feet,
may the strength of stone hold you firm.
When lack and scarcity pinch your life,
may the rich green Earth nourish you.
When your body grows weak from exhaustion,
may the oak tree lend you strength.
When all seems lost,
may birdsong and sunlight give you hope.
When your soul quakes with anxiety,
may the Christ-Spirit enfold you,
and may Divine Love cast out all fear.

—Ellyn Sanna
Celtic Prayers for Times of Crisis

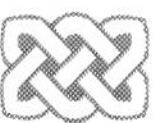

When anxiety grips me, heart and mind,
God of Love, comfort me and give me strength.

JULY 12

YOUR PRIVATE SANCTUARY

Of course, some seasons of life
make finding time to be alone with God difficult to schedule.
During those periods, seek out tiny quiet spaces in your life
and use them for drawing close to the Divine Presence
as frequently and habitually as you can.
It could be your daily commute to work . . .
it might be your morning shower . . .
it might be your bed in the moments before you sleep . . .
it might even be your bathroom!
Sometimes even an imaginary place in your mind can serve.
Claim that space as your personal hermitage,
your private sanctuary, where you make a habit of seeking God.
Wherever it is, God is waiting to meet with you.

—Kenneth McIntosh
Water from an Ancient Well

Divine One, show me places of sanctuary in my life,
where I can commune with you.

JULY 13

PATHS OF HEALING

There are many paths to healing and wholeness,
and many destinations as well.
We can pray for physical healing and the cessation of pain.
We may also receive healing
that awakens us to the pain of the world,
agitating our hearts before comforting our spirits,
as we identify with those who experience
injustice and intolerance.
Let us open to the healing we need in this moment.

—Bruce Epperly
101 Soul Seeds for Healing and Wholeness

Let every moment be a healing moment, Spirit.
May I find and spread your loving energy.

JULY 14

LIFE IS PRAYER

Because we live and move and have our being in God,
whether we realize it or not, we constantly pray.
I had heard that life is a prayer,
but I did not understand how this could be true.
Now I understand that I live in God.
I am always connected to God. I cannot disconnect,
even if I try. God's presence always remains.
Only my own awareness of God's presence comes and goes,
depending on the quality of my contemplation.

—Rich Lewis
Sitting with God

May I recognize today, Beloved One, that all of life is an opportunity to connect with you in prayer.

JULY 15

THE SECOND BOOK OF GOD

When you find yourself experiencing
a transcendent moment, don't talk,
don't reach for a camera, don't turn to anyone else
and try to get them to experience it too—
just be present.
These moments can occur anywhere, in a city,
out of a train window, on a mountain, in your garden.
The Second Book Of God is alive;
open it today and it reads differently to how it did yesterday.
I've personally never found real magic
in darkened rooms with mystical symbols,
but I have found it in the forest
or along the shore or in my back garden.

—Bruce Stanley
Forest Church

Teach me to see you and connect with you, Spirit,
in the world of Nature.

JULY 16

THE REALM OF HEAVEN NOW

Jesus changed the world forever each time he withstood
the force of the world's logic and expectations.
By doing the seemingly impossible, he proved that society,
tradition, politics, and government
need not have the final say. He said, "No!"
to injustice and poverty and hatred.
Jesus taught that the Realm of Heaven
is not the after-life but rather the now-life.
According to Jesus, the only rule that governs
this now-and-present Heaven is love (Matthew 22:37,39).
By refusing to obey this worlds' rules—
as demonstrated in his miracles—
he embodied a form of radical resistance
that can serve as a template for us all.

—Meg Llewellyn
Persistent Resistance

Help me, Spirit, to say no, as Jesus did,
to injustice wherever it exists.

JULY 17

LIVING WATER

The Living Water brings refreshing
in a dry and barren land
where refreshment for my soul is sparse and hard to find.
I long for you, Spirit. I thirst for your living water.
May it flow from the wellspring of heaven
into the very depths of my being.
Refresh my soul and revive my life.
As the rains revive the land's plants,
so to you I look to revive my life
with your living water from heaven.
Quench my thirst, I pray.

—David Cole
Celtic Prayers & Practices

Water of Life, restore the dry and wilted places
in my soul.

JULY 18

BREAK THE TEACUPS

Give me the courage, Beloved,
to let You drag me by the hair,
ripping from my hands all the toys that bring me no real joy.
Sometimes, Beloved, I know You get tired
of speaking to me sweetly.
You want to rip to shreds all my ideas about what truth is,
all the ideas that make me fight
within myself and with others, making the world weep
on days when it should be laughing. . . .
Hold me upside down, and shake all the nonsense out of me.
I'm in Your hands, Beloved. Shake me all You want.
Break all my tidy teacups
so that I'll have no more religious tea parties
where I sit there making conversation about You.

—Hafiz

Love Prayers

Spirit of Love, I trust you.
Do what you will with my life.

JULY 19

A CREATURE OF TWO WORLDS

What do I cherish most?
When it comes down to it, it's this—
the Love that makes my life limitless,
even in this world,
for my life is like a lotus:
it lives in the water, and it blossoms in the water,
and yet the water never touches its petals,
for they open above the water, beyond its reach.
I too am a creature of two worlds,
living in this one,
yet blossoming in the other.

—Kabîr
You're Already Home

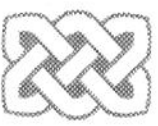

No matter what happens in this life, remind me, Spirit, that my life extends beyond into a far larger reality.

JULY 20

HEALTHY BOUNDARIES

We need to keep healthy boundaries
within our own bodies,
for we are called to be vessels of light
Fear drives us to seek self-medication,
sometimes unwisely, in the forms of drugs,
extreme behaviors, or sexually self-destructive activities.
In moments of temptation, we need to envision
our internal star, blazing with energy, able to burn away
the dross of self-loathing and inner doubt.
We are called out from forces of bondage
to become their true selves.

—Kenneth McIntosh
Hope in an Age of Fear

Show me, Spirit of Life, where to set boundaries
to protect my true Self.

JULY 21

MORE THAN WE CAN IMAGINE

We are Divine vitality, our hearts energized
by the Heartbeat of the Universe. We are world-shapers,
and the path to planetary transformation
begins with the intersection of our spirits
with the Spirit of the Universe, which gives birth to us
and this wondrous and dynamic Universe.
We are more than we can imagine, and so is everyone else.
Divine change moving the Universe bids us to move as well,
to grow into people who are more than we can imagine.
Behold, you are standing on Holy Ground.
Behold, you are Holy Ground.

—Bruce Epperly
101 Soul Seeds of Healing and Wholeness

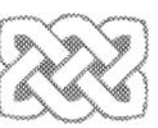

May your Heart beat within me, Spirit,
making me a child of the Universe
and a companion to all Creation.

JULY 22

CIRCLE PRAYER

Circle of love, encompass my loved ones.
May your love well up within them.
May your passion enlighten them.
Circle of healing, encompass my loved ones.
May your healing touch rest upon them.
May your light illumine them.
Circle of protection, encompass my loved ones.
Surround them with your eternal safety.
Protect them from all temptations and ills.
Give them courage and strength
to live always from your safe and powerful center.

—Bruce Epperly
Celtic Prayers for Times of Crisis

I give you the people I love, Life-Giver,
knowing you love them even more than I do.

JULY 23

ALREADY HOME

We suffer from multiple personality disorder—
every one of us.
We were each conceived as one, as a oneness.
We floated in amniotic fluid
with every wish fulfilled instantly.
Then we entered the world of differentiation,
of discrimination: this and that,
here and there, me and you, us and them.
We are no longer unified. We have even divided
the world into the spiritual and the physical.
No separation exists, but we have made it so.
The solution? To open to the awareness
that we are inseparable from the vast interconnecting
and ever-changing Sphere of Being.
In reality, we are always already home, safe, sound,
secure, ever-changing, and adventuring.

—George Breed
The Hidden Words of Jesus

Open my eyes, Spirit of Life, to the reality
that I am always, already home in you.

JULY 24

CONVERSATIONS WITH NATURE

Being in Nature, we become aware
of the attraction and pull we feel
at a deep soul level toward Nature's beauty.
The exploration of that attraction can become a dialogue,
And odd as it might seem, these conversations,
with elements of Nature—
such as a tree or rock or waterfall or bird—
can be illuminating, surprising and enriching.
I had a conversation once with a canyon;
in my conversation it seemed polite to mostly listen,
because what it had to say was very slow and deep.
I think I'm still waiting for it to finish its first sentence.

—Bruce Stanley
Forest Church

Teach me, Spirit of Life,
to listen to the slow, deep voice of Nature.

JULY 25

UNCONDITIONAL LOVE

Divine love is so completely unconditional
that God sees only our perfection.
Perfection? The very word seemed impossible
in connection with my so very-imperfect self,
and yet slowly, I came to understand
that my innermost being is perfect;
that the image of God is in me,
and nothing can destroy or mar or limit it.
Regardless of all my nonsense, depravity, cruelty, and pride,
a place exists inside me that remains pure and whole.

—Marietta Bahri Della Penna
Song of a Christian Sufi

Thank you, Beloved,
that your love is unconditional.

JULY 26

THE SONG NEVER ENDS

Listen, my friend.
Your body is God's harp.
God tightens the strings and plays love's melody.
When the strings snap and the pedals grow slack,
the harp will return to dust, for it was dust all along.
But the song was God's,
and the song never ends.

—Kabîr
You're Already Home

When I am afraid of death and life's other changes,
remind me, Beloved, that your song is eternal.

JULY 27

THE REALM OF SPIRIT

When we are already born into the Kingdom—
when we are Kingdom residents,
spirits in the realm of Spirit, energy-beings amid Energy—
to focus on fasting, praying, and giving to charity would be like
crawling on our hands and knees once we've learned to walk.
The skills we learned on our hands and knees
are incorporated into our walking—
but we need no longer practice those skills,
for we have internalized them.
As Mister Buddha said, once you reach the other shore,
You don't carry your boat around on your head.

—George Breed
The Hidden Words of Jesus

Show me, Spirit, when I am ready to internalize
the spiritual disciplines and begin to walk, run, fly.

JULY 28

AT HOME IN THE SPIRIT

Help us, Great Christ-Spirit,
to live in you as fish live in water,
soar with you as birds fly in air,
run for you as deer run in woods,
flow with you as water flows in streams,
blaze for you as twigs burn in fire.

—Ray Simpson
Tree of Life

In you, Spirit, I live and move
and have my being.

JULY 29

FULLY PRESENT

Out of the burning bush,
God calls Moses by name (Exodus 3:4),
and Moses responds, "Here am I."
He is fully present, both spiritually and geographically.
"The place where you are standing is holy ground,"
God tells Moses. Note that this holy location
is not a building constructed with hands or machinery,
not a center of social and political events,
but a patch of ground
on a remote mountain in the wilderness.
Alone with God.

—Lynne Bundesen
The Feminine Spirit

May I be fully present today, Living One,
so I don't overlook the "burning bushes" in my life.

JULY 30

SELFISHNESS

When Jesus told his followers, "If you want to follow me,
you're going to have to take up your cross,"
he was speaking metaphorically;
he didn't mean all his followers should lug around
a literal cross on their shoulders,
the way he eventually would have to do.
Instead, he was saying we cannot grow spiritually
without learning to let go of our selfishness,
our need to have our own way,
to put ourselves at the center of the world.

—Kenneth McIntosh
Water from an Ancient Well

Divine Child, may I accept the "crosses" in my life.
Free me from the need to put my ego first.

JULY 31

QUESTIONS

It is said that Saint Francis passed an entire night
asking two simple questions:
Who are you, God?
Who am I, God?
Many people would have us
rush through to the answers.
There is power and wisdom
in sitting with these questions.

—Jeff Campbell
Discovering the Essence

Expand my understanding, Living One,
of both you and myself.

AUGUST 1

LAMMAS DAY

SUMMER THANKSGIVING

In the heat and haze of early August,
Lord, I praise Your Holy Name,
For this first harvest of tomatoes from my garden.
For the warm, brown earth they have grown from:
I give thanks to the Creator.
For the thundery summer rain that watered them:
I give thanks to the Child.
For the hot summer sun that has ripened the fruit:
I give thanks to the Spirit.
Each deep red globe,
gently twisted from under scented leaves,
a small miracle to hold in my own hand.
By Your bounteous grace, O Lord, and the sweat of my brow,
I have partnered with You in this miracle.
All praise to You, God of the green and growing Earth!
All praise to You, God of rain and sun and fruitfulness!
All praise to You, God of my backyard tomato harvest!

—Bill Palmer
Earth Afire with God

The ancient celebration of Lammas Day (called *Lughnasadh* in the Pagan calendar) is a holy day of thanksgiving for Earth's abundance.

AUGUST 2

ENRICHING THE EARTH

We offer You the Earth
and the vegetables that grow from it,
for all creation is Yours,
and we want to be enriching it, not abusing it.
We offer You the Earth
and the minerals that lie within it,
for all creation is Yours,
and we want to be enriching it, not exploiting it.
We offer You the Earth
and the birds and beasts that live upon it;
for all creation is Yours,
and we want to be enriching it, not betraying it.
We offer You ourselves
who make our home upon this Earth,
for all creation is Yours, and we want to be enriching it.

—Ray Simpson
Dance of Creation

Remind me, Creator, to give back to you—
with honor and care—the Earth that is already yours.

AUGUST 3

MAKE JUSTICE COME ALIVE

Love of Christ, breathe in me.
Unite me with your human Body.
Reveal anything in me that blocks the flow of your love.
Show me practical ways I can work
to make your Body stronger.
Bring new people and relationships into my life.
May we together set the world on fire,
making love and justice come alive.

—Patrick Saint-Jean, SJ
The Spiritual Work of Racial Justice

Use me, Spirit of Life, to bring justice to the world.

AUGUST 4

FLOATING IN THE SEA OF GOD

I'd be silly, Beloved,
to say that You are something separate,
something "out there,"
when all the while,
You're all around me.
It would be like floating in the sea
and insisting
that there's no water touching me,
that water is not pressing gently
against every inch of my skin.

—Hafiz
Love Prayers

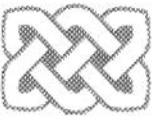

Thank you, Spirit of Love,
that even if I am often unaware,
you always surround me.

AUGUST 5

SUMMER GRATITUDE

High King, O Bright One with the Strong Hand,
You are at our door.
Come in!
Shining One, World Wright, Harper and Hero,
Star Smith, Lord of the Grain,
You are at our door.
Come in!
Lord of the Grain, You surrender to the sickle.
You surrender to the earth. You surrender to death.
Lord of Life, Shining One, High King,
take your queen, Queen of the Grain, Lady of the Summer,
Mother of the Field, Giver of Bread.
We thank you!

—Meg Llewellyn
The Celtic Wheel of the Year

Thank You, Giver of Life,
for the abundance and beauty of summer.

AUGUST 6

SITTING WITH GOD

Here is what I hear God say:
"I am Presence. Go ahead and sit with Me.
Go ahead and ask Me questions.
I am always with you.
My peace is always with you.
I am in everything: people, earth,
trees, mountains, waters.
I love you.
Be present wherever you are.
Listen and observe. Use all of your senses.
Love others. Do not judge.
Sit with Me. Ask Me questions.
Wait for the answers."

—Rich Lewis
Sitting with God

Give me the patience, Holy One,
to simply sit with you, present to all that is.

AUGUST 7

THIN PLACES

The Celts knew Nature was their portal
to a great spiritual reality.
Wells, mountain crags, caves, and lochs were "thin places"
that allowed access to the realm of Spirit.
In these temples of Nature, the Celts sought
physical and spiritual healing, as well as revelation.
The salmon, the eagle, and even the tiny hazelnut,
all were allies in helping humanity access
the mysterious magic that underlies physical matter.

—Kenneth McIntosh
Water from an Ancient Well

Attune me to your Presence, Spirit,
in the natural world around me.
May I never be too busy to notice you.

AUGUST 8

PEACE

Lord of all peace,
who calmed the storms of the seas,
bring calm to my soul, engulf me in your peace,
which is beyond my understanding,
that I may feel safe from the wilds of this world
and from those of the spirit realm.
Prince of Peace, come reign in me
with the peace only you can bring,
the peace that draws me
to a state of inner bliss with myself,
with the world around me, and with you.
Keep me from panic and irrational fear;
keep me from anxiety and worry;
keep me from dwelling on negativity.
Stay my soul with your steadfast security.
Keep me calm and at peace.

—David Cole
Celtic Prayers & Practices

Thank you, Beloved One,
that you always hold me steady.

AUGUST 9

LONELINESS

I'm so lonely.
I don't know who I am.
I've lost my very self,
and I don't have a clue who You are.
I'm nothing in this world,
and I've made no progress in the spiritual world.
"Sweetheart," you whisper in my ear,
"I'm right here.
Listen to your breath.
That's Me."

—Khajah Abdullah Ansari
Love Prayers

When I'm discouraged and lonely,
remind me, Holy One,
that you are already as close as my breath.

AUGUST 10

ROOTED IN FAITH, HOPE, AND LOVE

Our Protector Jesus chooses to be intimate with us
in utter simplicity, humility, and courtesy.
Christ is the embodiment of Divine intimacy with humanity.
This amazing joy belongs to each of us.
In my opinion, this is the most complete joy
we shall ever know: the astounding familiarity and hospitality
God our Maker and Christ our Brother
and Rescuer extend to us.
None of us can completely experience
this marvelous intimacy in this life—
but we can claim it in faith and love,
for it is in faith, hope, and love
that our lives are rooted and made firm.

—Julian of Norwich
All Shall Be Well

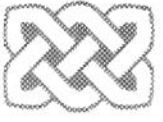

I am grateful, humbled, full of joy that I can be intimate with you, Life-Giver, rooted in the love we share.

AUGUST 11

THE SUN

The eye of the great God,
the eye of the God of glory,
the eye of the Creator of hosts,
the eye of the God of the living,
pouring upon us,
pouring upon us gently and generously,
glory to you, O glorious sun!
Glory to you,
the face of the God of life!

—adapted from the *Carmina Gadelica*
The Celtic Wheel of the Year

Each time I see the sun, Spirit of Life,
may I open myself to your life-giving light.

AUGUST 12

NATURE'S TRUTH

Vines twirl and swirl across our property lines.
Like all of Nature, they are no respecter of human boundaries.
Those imaginary lines we draw between properties
(and between nations) exist only in our minds.
Nature knows better.
Nature has no sense of "mine."

—Melina Rudman
Sacred Soil

Show me the unnatural boundaries I've drawn, Spirit,
lines that keep you and your living world
separated from me.

AUGUST 13

BREATHING GOD'S NAME

Many rabbis believe that YHWH—God's name—
was, in fact, never meant to be said at all.
Instead, these specific letters,
emulate the act of breathing itself.
If this understanding is right,
then God does not belong to the category of things
to which we give word-sound names.
And yet, in that act of breathing, we say God's name
hundreds of times each day.
We say God's name slowly in times of calm.
We chant God's name quickly, desperately,
in times of panic or ecstasy.
It was the first thing we did when we were born.
It will be the last thing we do before we die.

—Jeff Campbell
Discovering the Essence

Remind me today, Life-Giver,
that each breath I breathe speaks your name.

AUGUST 14

EAGLE WINGS

"You have seen . . . how I bore you
on eagle's wings and brought you to me,"
says God in the Book of Exodus.
In this verse, in the masculine-gendered eagle
with feminine-gendered wings,
we see how Mother-Father God
is defined as both feminine and masculine,
as well as the "I AM," sheer Being beyond gender,
the One who does all things—unlimited,
impossible to confine, immediate, present.
In this Mothering and Fathering,
we find eternal, forever consciousness.

—Lynne Bundesen
The Feminine Spirit

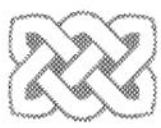

Help me, Spirit, to see you revealed in all gender forms,
even as you are also beyond all gender.

AUGUST 15

EVERY BREATH A PRAYER

Every breath can be a prayer
if I devote my breaths to God and neighbor,
including during my interactions on social media.
I breathe and open to insight when I log onto my computer.
I breathe gently and deeply when I experience myself
becoming stressed or busy while responding
to professional e-mail communications.
I breathe before I post any response on Facebook.
I breathe as I gaze at images on Facebook.
When confronted with anger and hostility online,
I breathe in God's peace and choose not to respond.

—Bruce Epperly
God Online

Breathe on me, Breath of God,
so that my every action
brings joy and healing to every living being.

AUGUST 16

GOD IS HERE

Busy as we are with worries and fears
about both the past and the future,
humans often miss the opportunities they have
to hear what God has to say.
Rumi, perhaps the greatest of the Sufi poets,
wrote: "Each moment contains a hundred messages from God.
To every cry of 'Oh Lord,' He answers a hundred times,
'I am here.'" I was finally learning to listen
to a voice I had nearly forgotten existed.

—Marietta Bahri Della Penna
Song of a Christian Sufi

Beloved, help me today
to hear your voice more clearly.

AUGUST 17

MENTAL IMAGES

When hold on to a limited image of God,
when we place our trust in these mental constructs,
we are not necessarily trusting God;
instead, we are trusting our *ideas* about God.
The journey of deepening trust in God
peels away these ideas we held so dearly and closely.
This can feel painful, but the concepts that fall away
are like old layers of skin we have now outgrown;
we are like snakes that need to shed
their outer epidermis in order to grow.

—Sharon Grussendorff
Deeper

Shed your light, Spirit, so I can see
the ideas and images of you
that restrict rather than free me.

AUGUST 18

WHOLENESS

Lead us from that which binds to that which frees;
lead us from that which cramps to that which creates;
lead us from that which lies to that which speaks truth;
lead us from that which blights to that which ennobles;
lead us from that which hides to that which celebrates;
lead us from that which fades to that which endures.
Lead us from showing off to showing love;
lead us from being unreal to being real;
lead us from that which is partial
to that which makes whole.

—Ray Simpson
Tree of Life

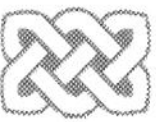

Today, Spirit, may I live in the freedom
and wholeness of your Presence.

AUGUST 19

VISION

With Vision, we are aware of the consciousness
that is the universe. Our world shifts from the prosaic,
from a bottom line to be constantly calculated,
to the poetry of that which births us,
that which is in constant communion with us,
that which nurtures us, challenges us,
brings us into fleshly existence . . . and out again.
We no longer confine ourselves to the cold eye of intellect
and the desirous eye of the body.
We must open our third eye,
the eye of Spirit, of the Life Force,
the eye that sees the beauty and harmony of the Cosmos.

—George Breed
The Hidden Words of Jesus

Open the eye of my spirit, Life Force,
so that I may see you.

AUGUST 20

FRUITS OF THE SPIRITUAL JOURNEY

As we face our own vulnerability and uncertainty,
we are less likely to coerce other people
to believe things our way or to judge others' behaviors.
Instead, as we wend our way ever more deeply
into the depth dimension, we begin
to experience a generous spaciousness and inner authority.
This is true transformation—and we
can recognize it by its fruits.
Galatians 5:22 describes these fruits as
"love, joy, peace, patience, kindness, generosity,
faithfulness, gentleness and self-control."
These speak with so much more clarity
than the thumping words many people
shout in the name of Jesus.
These spiritual "fruits" result from real inner transformation,
which is the work of God in us.

—Sharon Grussendorff

Deeper

Spirit of the Depths, may my life bear your fruit.

AUGUST 21

MAKING LOVE WITH THE DIVINE

Ever since I met my Beloved,
we have never stopped making love.
I don't shut my eyes when I pray,
I don't plug my ears,
I don't fast or practice any other discipline.
I simply look at the world
with my eyes open, smiling,
and I see Divine beauty everywhere.
Whatever I see, reminds me of God.
Whatever I do, becomes worship.
Day and night are the same for me;
all contradictions have become one.

—Kabîr
You're Already Home

Today, Beloved, may you and I make love
in each moment and in every circumstance.

AUGUST 22

STANDING FOR LOVE

In the old stories, Brigid, like Jesus,
tapped into a supernatural stream of power,
but the miracles she worked are not as important
as what they tell us about who she was
and what she stood for.
She stood for the poor, the vulnerable,
the broken, the outcast.
She stood for love and compassion and generosity.
She stood for God and the Divine Realm.
With each act of resistance,
she planted her feet firmly on Heaven's ground.

—Meg Llewellyn
Persistent Resistance

May I too, Spirit of Love,
take my stand on Heaven's ground.

AUGUST 23

WISE GARDENERS

Divine Source of Truth,
Beauty and Goodness,
our minds are like a field.
In this field, please grow many good things,
many beautiful things,
and many true things with deep roots.
Teach us also how to weed and sift and sort,
how to water and prune wisely.

—Ray Simpson
Tree of Life

Give me the discernment I need, Spirit of Truth,
to see what in my life needs to be water
and what needs to be pruned.

AUGUST 24

SELF-CARE

Care for your soul as well as your body.
Move your mind as well as your body.
Spend time in silence as well as physical exercise.
Perhaps even let your movement be meditation,
letting Wisdom flow through you
as your spiritual cardio charge.
Let the healing energy of God inspire each moment
and every encounter, transforming your soul
as well as your cells.

—Bruce Epperly
101 Soul Seeds of Healing and Wholeness

Remind me, Spirit, to feed my soul as well as my body,
to move my mind as well as my muscles.
Let Your Energy of Love animate every thought,
emotion, movement, and relationship.

AUGUST 25

SUMMER BLESSINGS

On this summer morn,
bless to me, O God, each thing my eyes see;
each fair tree and blooming flower;
each fragrant field and blue hill crest.
Bless to me, O God, each sound my ears hear;
each murmuring dove, each lowing cow,
each laughing child.
Bless to me, O God, each odor that goes in my nostrils,
the scent of green things growing.
Bless to me, O God,
each taste that goes into my lips,
the sweetness of milk and honey.
Bless to me each note that makes my song;
each ray of light that guides my way.

—adapted from the *Carmina Gadelica*
The Celtic Wheel of the Year

Thank You, Living One,
that you reveal yourself in each experience of my senses.

AUGUST 26

MY LIFE'S DIRECTION

Thank you, Life-Giver,
for the deeply woven roots of life.
Thank you for those who have been my parents,
mentors, kin, siblings, and companions.
Thank you for the good Earth from which I come.
Let me be known as a good ancestor
to those who follow me,
one who loves the Earth and protects all life.

—Bruce Epperly
From Cradle to Cosmos

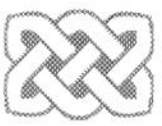

Thank you, Spirit, for the web of life
that connects me to both the past and the future.

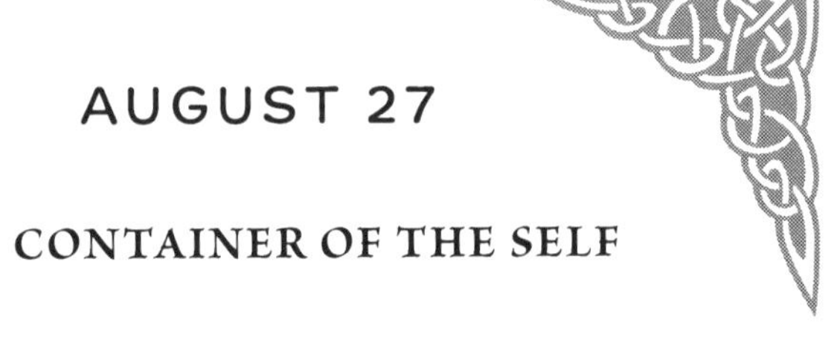

AUGUST 27

THE CONTAINER OF THE SELF

During the first half of life, we build the container of the self.
We learn to do what is right, we try to be successful
at our work and in our families, but at
some point, this container
necessarily begins to crack, as we realize life
is so much more painful and messy
than our formulas or beliefs can explain.
This cracking is an opportunity for growth.
The gaping contradictions, questions, and messiness of life
present us with opportunities to allow ourselves to gradually,
bit by bit, let go of the container of the self,
so we can wake up to who we really are—
the Self we are in union with God,
the Self who is filled with the light of the knowledge of God.

—Sharon Grussendorff
Deeper

Give me the courage to break, Living One,
so that I can grow into my true Self.

AUGUST 28

THE ORDINARY

I realized I was being asked to rethink
the way I looked at the spiritual life.
I loved the unconventional, the esoteric,
and yes, even at times, the bizarre.
But the Divine One is to be found in the ordinary,
the mundane, the everyday tasks.
Whether we realize it or not, whether we like it or not,
God is found there besides us, within us,
in the midst of daily life.

—Marietta Bahri Della Penna
Song of a Christian Sufi

Teach me, Divine One, to see you
in the ordinary circumstances of my life.

AUGUST 29

SELFHOOD

Selfhood is not something we ever achieve once and forever.
Some of us may be farther along than others are
on the continuum of inner strength,
but all of us are still growing.
If life's crises makes us aware that we lack courage,
that our inner core is easily thrown off balance,
that self-knowledge can be the first step toward growth.
As we pray for strength and courage,
we give the Divine One opportunity to work within us,
lifting us up to new heights.

—Ellyn Sanna
Celtic Prayers for Times of Crises

Guide me, Spirit, on the path to selfhood.

AUGUST 30

AN INTIMATE, EXPERIENTIAL GOD

I have moved from experiencing God
As Someone in the sky looking down upon us
to my present understanding of God as Presence.
I now experience Divine Presence as accessible at all times,
and particularly accessible in silence.
This is a huge shift, from distant to intimate,
From abstract to experiential.

—Rich Lewis
Sitting with God

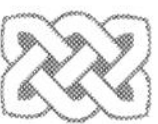

Break the boxes I've kept you in, Life-Giver,
so I can learn to experience
your real and intimate Presence.

AUGUST 31

DETACHMENT

Detachment is essential to a mystic path of spirituality,
but when the mystics spoke of detachment,
they did not mean we are to detach from the world
in the sense that we no longer care about what's going on it.
When we hear about injustice in our communities,
we are not to meekly fold our hands
and mouth pious platitudes about God's will.
Instead, the challenge is to detach from our own egos—
the selfishness within our hearts that insists
we come first, that we deserve to have our own way,
that our lives matter more than others'—
so that we are free to take action on behalf of justice.
This detachment allows us to act with clarity and humility,
unencumbered by self-interest and pride.

—Ellyn Sanna
Persistent Resistance

Help me, Holy One, to detach from my ego,
so that I am free to take action and defend justice.

SEPTEMBER 1

NEW BEGINNINGS

As I move through this stage in life,
leaving the past to start anew,
I pray your guidance and protection
on all I am and have to do.
Cause fear to be not within my soul
as I make this transition with you,
as I take the path you have lain before me.
I pass through this gateway with confidence
that on life's journey I have you
with me as my guide.
So keep within me, through changes all,
clear sight of you and of your call.

—David Cole
Celtic Prayers & Practices

When I was young, Holy One,
September was the start of a new school year.
May this season still be a time of
new opportunities to grow.

SEPTEMBER 2

THE REIGN OF GOD

O God of Mercy,
we pray that we may be open
to your movement in our hearts,
so that we may hear the stories of others, and be inspired;
so that we may see the suffering of others,
and be compassionate;
so that we may understand others, and walk with them;
and so that, with the help of Christ
who taught us how to love,
we may do our part to make real your Reign.

—Patrick Saint-Jean, SJ
The Spiritual Work of Racial Justice

Merciful One, teach me to love as you love,
actively, unconditionally, without judgment.

SEPTEMBER 3

HARVEST TIME

Thank You for harvest's boundless store,
and the fruits of the Earth
that sustain and gladden us.
Thank You for those who work the land,
for each part of the food chain
that reaches to our door.
Thank You for comforts of life
and the power to help others.
Thank You for Your creation
and the life that sings in our blood.

—Ray Simpson
The Dance of Creation

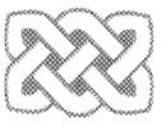

Remind me, Spirit of Life, to see your movement
in the ordinary details of life.
May I not take anything for granted.

SEPTEMBER 4

GOD IS SINGING IN YOUR SOUL

Next time you're praying,
picture a shrine within your soul.
It could be a temple or a church or a mosque.
That doesn't matter. What matters is the light.
Step inside your soul shrine.
See the way the light streams through the windows,
filling the entire place with light?
Now step outside the shrine.
See the way the light streams out from the windows
so everyone can see?
Now listen.
Can you hear from inside the shrine
the sound of someone singing?
That's God worshiping inside the shrine
inside your soul.

—Marietta Bahri Della Penna
Prayers of a Christian Sufi

Today, Beloved, may I hear your song inside me.

SEPTEMBER 5

OLD WAYS

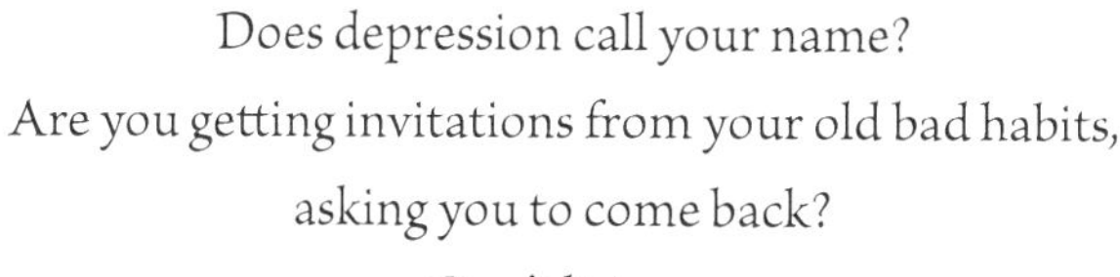

Does depression call your name?
Are you getting invitations from your old bad habits,
asking you to come back?
Don't listen.
Instead, keep squeezing new light
from the sunshine,
from your work and prayer, from music,
and from every glance from the Beloved.
Stop trying to buy life with counterfeit money.
Sweetheart, if you go back to your old ways,
you'll be like someone
tied to the back end of a farting pig.
Instead, learn what delights the Beloved.
Those are the things that will bring you freedom and life.

—Hafiz

Love Prayers

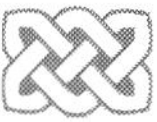

Help me, Divine Energy, to leave the past behind,
so that I can live in your joy.

SEPTEMBER 6

ENVIRONMENTAL JUSTICE

A renewed relationship with the Earth
is not an optional aspect of faith in Christ;
it is an urgent necessity. Our species is a threat
to "all our relations" with whom we share the planet.
Followers of Jesus are called to commit themselves
To Christ's desire that God's will be
done "on earth, as in heaven."
The Spirit within impels us to address injustice
wherever it takes place.

—Kenneth McIntosh
Water from an Ancient Well

Show me ways, Spirit, I need to change
and actions I need to take,
so I can help to heal the Earth.

SEPTEMBER 7

WHAT YOU CAN'T CONTROL

You know, Spirit,
how I hate to surrender my control;
how much I want to say, "Mine!"
Teach me to make peace
with what I can't control.
Remind me to make room in my life
for the uncontrollable, the unknowable,
for You.

—Melina Rudman
Sacred Soil

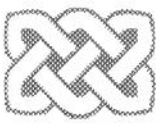

I give to you, Spirit of the Universe,
my entire life.
Make it grow.

SEPTEMBER 8

MARYMASS

THE COMPANIONSHIP OF MARY

Mary the fragrant,
Mother of the Shepherd of the flocks,
today I go sunways around my dwelling,
in your name, Mary Mother,
who has preserved me through summer heat,
and will preserve me,
through autumn wind and winter cold,
in peace, in sufficiency, in work, in love,
in wisdom, in mercy, for the sake of Your Son,
the Christ of all grace.
Till the day of my death, do not forsake me!
Till the day of my death, you will not forsake me!

—adapted from the *Carmina Gadelica*
The Celtic Wheel of the Year

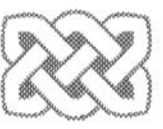

The Celts lived in a friendly universe,
where both the dead and the living
continued to work together in love.
Mary, the mother of Jesus,
was a treasured friend in their journeys through life.

SEPTEMBER 9

THE DIVINE BODY

Humanity finds its saving life in unity.
For God is everything that is good;
the Divine One has made and loves all reality.
This is the Body,
and when a human being loves others in that Body,
she is loving all Creation.
Contained within redeemed humanity is everything—
all Creation and its Maker—for God is in humanity,
and God is in all, and so everything is united
into a single Body.

—Julian of Norwich
All Shall Be Well

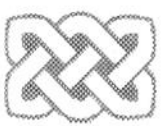

Creator, today may I honor
and treasure your Body, in all its forms.

SEPTEMBER 10

NONDUALISM

I was taught, "Here are the humans. There is God."
This is called theism.
It is the primal dualism, the ultimate either/or.
Dualism tells us that X can be inside of Y:
my milk carton can be inside that paper bag over there.
Or Y can be inside of X:
we could crumple up the paper bag
and put it inside the milk carton.
Nondualism says maybe the same bag
can both be inside of the milk carton
and outside of it at the same time.

—Jeff Campbell
Discovering the Essence

You are both all around me, Life-Giver,
and also inside me.

SEPTEMBER 11

SHEKINAH

Medieval Jewish Bible scholars believed that
when the Hebrews endured the agonies of slavery
and the hardships of the wilderness,
they did not do so alone, because Shekinah,
the feminine aspect of God, dwelled alongside them.
These thirteenth-century mystics
portrayed the feminine Shekinah as a loving mother
who suffers with her children and is manifested,
literally and physically, through a woman's body.
This Feminine Spirit is who brings the Hebrews
out of suffering, slavery, and oppression.

—Lynne Bundesen
The Feminine Spirit

May your light, Shekinah, lead us—
both individually and as a society—
out of oppression and into freedom.

SEPTEMBER 12

LOVE ONLINE

Can I speak the truth with love
in the context of social media incivility and fabrication?
Whenever I communicate, whether my words
are prophetic, mundane, or perfunctory,
I have begun to prayerfully ponder every post,
asking if my posts come from a place of love or fear,
friendship or anger, help or harm.
As I post, I affirm:
"I share this post with great love for all who notice it."

—Bruce Epperly
God Online

Let my ordinary interaction online
become windows to Divinity.
May they bring healing and wholeness to the world.

SEPTEMBER 13

THE REAL IS YOUR HOME

Whenever I hear about fish in the river
who think they are thirsty, I burst out laughing.
You're no different from those fish.
Don't you see that the Real is your home,
and you are already there?
But you wander here and there, bored with your life,
always searching somewhere else for meaning.
Let me tell you something.
It doesn't matter if you travel to Paris or Timbuctoo;
if you don't find your own soul,
everything you see will seem unreal.

—Kabîr

You're Already Home

Remind me, Spirit of Life, that I won't find you
by searching restlessly in the external world,
not until I find you in my own soul.

SEPTEMBER 14

INCARNATING THE PRESENCE OF THE DIVINE

The sun shines. The Pleiades illumine.
Pacific Ocean waters roar.
Sycamore branches extend into the sky.
Bright white and yellow daisies bloom.
Jaguars roam, hunt, and eat.
These nonhuman creations are free to fully express
what the Creator wants them to be!
God is within all that exists, from the Milky Way galaxy
to the tiniest atom in a squirrel's tail.
And God is within me. I can decide to respond
to this Love that is within me; I can choose to let it flow
out of me and into the world in inspired words and deeds.

—Rich Lewis
Sitting with God

May I, like all other living things,
learn to fully express your Presence within me.

SEPTEMBER 15

YOU SHINE!

In your mind's eye,
see what is overcast and storm-covered in your world,
the creeping shadow of fear.
And then see yourself as a lamp,
a sparkling jewel, a star.
See your brightness overwhelm the dark forces around you.
Your imagination is not some childish thing;
what you envision inwardly
will shine outwardly into the world,
cutting fear down to size and leading others to hope.

—Kenneth McIntosh
Hope in an Age of Fear

Thank you, Spirit of Life,
that you shine in me.

SEPTEMBER 16

FEAST DAY OF SAINT NINIAN

EXPLORERS

Blessed Ninian,
we ask that you walk with us
as we, like you,
journey to unknown lands,
places we have not yet explored,
thoughts and ideas that are unfamiliar.
Share with us your courage,
your dedication, your fidelity and love.
Blessed Ninian, walk with us.

—Meg Llewellyn
The Celtic Wheel of the Year

In the fourth century, Ninian left his homeland to bring the Good News of God's love through Christ to the Picts who lived in what is now Scotland.

SEPTEMBER 17

TREASURED

God says to me,
"Stop building all those traps around yourself.
Burst free like a lion from a cage.
Worship Me as if you could see Me
with your physical eyes.
You are blind to Me, but I see you.
You have broken faith with Me
and with yourself,
but I still keep faith with you;
I am truer to you than you are to yourself;
I treasure you more than you do yourself."

—Sanai

Love Prayers

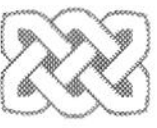

Thank you, Beloved, for your faithfulness to me.
Thank you for your unconditional and limitless love.

SEPTEMBER 18

BEGINNING AND ENDING

We are always here at the beginning,
where everything has its start.
All creation flows out of NOW.
No other place exists but Now.
Beginnings and endings interflow,
allowing an ongoing cycle of change.
We live in a continuous flow
of ending-beginning-ending-beginning.
We ourselves are always ending-beginning-ending-beginning.
When we truly know this and are this,
something amazing happens.

—George Breed
The Hidden Words of Jesus

When all I see is endings, Spirit,
remind me they are also beginnings.

SEPTEMBER 19

BELOVED BODIES

To recognize that God loves our bodies
challenges us to affirm the bodies of others,
treating others' bodies with respect.
Loving God in the world of the flesh challenges us
to treat everyone as a sibling,
honoring humanity through ethical relationships.
Affirming the bodies of others also means
working to ensure that everyone has adequate nourishment,
housing, health care, and a healthy environment.
Let us rejoice in our embodiment and claim our vocation
to nurture the bodies of our siblings.

—Bruce Epperly
101 Soul Seeds of Healing and Wholeness

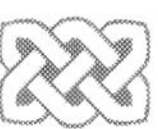

I thank You, Spirit, for the wonder of embodiment.
I commit myself to honor my own body
and to treat all bodies with respect.

SEPTEMBER 20

DYING IN ORDER TO LIVE

The step-by-step dying process is also mysteriously,
step-by-step, a life-giving process.
The death-resurrection pattern is lived out
in a spiral kind of way in our own lives,
as a gradual unwrapping of the gift of who we are.
Each time we let go of our will,
surrendering to God's higher way,
we weaken the false self's grip on our sense of who we are
As we practice letting go, we will discover
in increasing depth and continuity who we are in God.

—Sharon Grussendorff
Deeper

Remind me today, Life-Giver, to let go of my false self,
so that I discover who I truly am in you.

SEPTEMBER 21

FREE TO LOVE AND BE LOVED

God is love (1 John 4:8). And God is within me.
When I forget this, I live in fear and worry.
I am afraid to take on new tasks and afraid
to experience unfamiliar things. I lack confidence.
When I forget that God is love and God is within me,
I often make the wrong choices.
Or I make no choice. I freeze. I stop movement forward.
I procrastinate. I complain. I blame others. I'm unhappy.
As soon as I remember that God is within me, though,
I no longer have any reason to fear.
I am free—free to explore. I am free to experience life,
free to love and be loved.

—Rich Lewis
Sitting with God

May I find in your love
the freedom to be my true Self.

SEPTEMBER 22

AUTUMN EQUINOX (MABON)

BALANCE

Help us, Mother God,
to find the balance of Mabon.
Teach us that for all that is dark, there is light;
for all that is bad, there is good;
for all that causes sorrow,
there is that which causes joy;
and for all that falls,
there is new rising, each in its time.
May we find Your balance,
Mother God, in our lives, and in our hearts.
Prepare us for winter's dark.
May we rest in You, unafraid.

—Meg Llewellyn
The Celtic Wheel of the Year

Mothering Spirit,
may I rest in your holy balance.

SEPTEMBER 23

OLD HABITS

Our souls' old habits of thought
are created by society and culture,
by education and family, by many voices coming at us
from outside our deepest, truest selves.
The soul's dark nights strip these habits from us
leaving us naked and afraid,
with nothing familiar to hold on to.
The external things that once made us happy—
money, prestige, material success,
the comfort of others' voices telling us who we are—
no longer satisfy us. In desperation,
we are driven deeper into the darkness, into ourselves.
The spiritual journey always leads into the dark—
and life is found there.

—Marietta Bahri Della Penna
Song of a Christian Sufi

Help me, Beloved, to be comfortable in the dark,
knowing you are there with me.

SEPTEMBER 24

GOD INCARNATED IN THE EARTH

Christ incarnates (becomes flesh) in all creation.
If God is incarnate in Nature,
then Earth-care is ministry to God's own being,
worship in every sense of the word.
Since all the world's creatures incarnate Christ,
we can apply Jesus' words (in Matthew 25:40) to the Earth:
"Whatever you do unto the Earth—its atmosphere,
Its plants, its creatures, and all your fellow humans
across the face of the globe—you do unto me."
We live in a world where God reveals the miracle of grace
in sky and leaf and stone. Even the tiny droplets of water in
a rainbow color the world with their
message of God's faithfulness.
All creation invites us to the joy of God's presence.
If enough people embraced these Celtic attitudes,
which are both deeply spiritual and intensely practical,
it could result in the salvation of our very planet.

—Kenneth McIntosh
Water from an Ancient Well

May I see you, Divine Spirit, incarnated everywhere,
and may I never cease to honor and protect
your Presence in the world.

SEPTEMBER 25

TRAVELING LIGHT

Help us to travel light, Holy One,
and so to know joys of discovery.
Help us to shed prejudice,
and so to be strangers no longer
but pilgrims together.
Help us to stop trying to control,
and so to let things happen
and to find you in the journeying.

Ray Simpson
Tree of Life

Help me today, Holy One, to follow you.
Strip my prejudices away.
Make me willing to be surprised by your light
shining in all people and places.

SEPTEMBER 26

HARMONY BETWEEN THE VISIBLE AND THE INVISIBLE

Awen is both a modern-day Pagan notion
and an ancient one that dates back
to at least the eighth century (and probably far earlier).
The Welsh word is often translated as "creative inspiration,"
but it has a much deeper meaning having to do
with a transformed relationship between
inner and outer reality.
The person adept at awen was called an *awenydd*,
someone who returned from her mystical experiences
with down-to-earth patterns for
harmonizing the entire community
with the visible world as well as the invisible Otherworld.

—Marjorie Bennett
Persistent Resistance

Spirit, show me practical ways to bring harmony between this world and the Otherworld.

SEPTEMBER 27

USED BY GOD

O Holy Mystery, all-loving God,
open my heart to hear your Voice
through the cries of a wounded world,
to see your Face in the midst of a darkened world.
O Holy Mystery, all-healing God,
use me to repair a broken world,
to speak truth in the midst of confusion,
bringing comfort to a world of sorrow.
O Holy Mystery, do your will, work your way,
unseen, unheard, in the midst of our wounded world,
in the midst of our darkened world,
in the midst of our broken world.

—Ellyn Sanna
Celtic Prayers for Times of Crisis

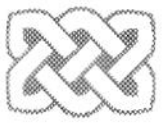

Use me, Holy Mystery,
to bring your love to the world.

SEPTEMBER 28

WOMB LOVE

A powerful biblical feminine image of God occurs
when, pronouncing Divine identity,
one of the words used derives
from a root noun that means, literally, "womb"
(although the word has usually been translated
as "merciful" or "compassionate").
We could say, then, that God loves us
with "womb-love," the love of a pregnant mother
for her yet-to-be-born child.
References to Divine womb-love
can be found over and over.

—Lynne Bundesen
Feminine Spirit

Thank you, Divine One,
for both your mother love and your father love.

SEPTEMBER 29

MICHAELMAS

ANGELIC PROTECTION

Michael, angel of glory,
bless all things that come together:
all rivers that meet and flow as one;
all milk and eggs and butter
beaten together in the bowl,
all harvest fruit and grain,
in the name of God the Son,
who gave them growth in summer's sun.
On this autumn morn,
I kneel at your footstool, Michael bright warrior.
Be a sanctuary all around me.

—adapted from the *Carmina Gadelica*
The Celtic Wheel of the Year

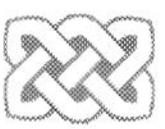

The Celts consider the angels to be
their friends and helpers,
and they especially treasured their
relationship with Michael,
the great warrior of heaven.

SEPTEMBER 30

SIMPLY

Listen, seeker!
Practice self-discipline, but do it simply.
As the seed is within the tree,
and within the seed are flowers and fruit and shade,
in the same way, the seed of Life is within your body,
and within that seed, you'll find your body again.
Apart from God, you cannot breathe air,
drink water, or warm yourself at a fire,
for God is in all things.
You breathe God, you drink God,
and God warms you.

—Kabîr
You're Already Home

When I'm tempted to complicate life,
remind me, Beloved, that you are with me.

OCTOBER 1

CONTENTMENT

O sacred season of autumn,
be our teacher, for we wish to learn
the virtue of contentment.
As we gaze upon your full-coloured beauty
we sense all in you an at-home-ness
with your amber riches.
You are the season of retirement,
of full barns and harvested fields.
The cycle of growth has ceased
and the busy work of giving life is now completed.
We sense in you no regrets; for you have lived a full life.
May we learn from your example.

—Ray Simpson
The Dance of Creation

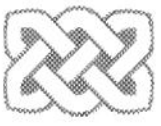

Creator, teach me autumn's wisdom.
Help me to let go.

OCTOBER 2

GROWING FEATHERS AND WINGS

In the dead of night, Beloved God,
I began to cry, because I finally understood:
the world in which I live is like a closed coffin.
I have lived my entire foolish, lonely life
inside this box.
When Death comes at last to lift the lid,
I'll spread my wings
and fly off into Eternity, just like a bird.
But Beloved, help me even now,
while the lid is still tight on my coffin,
to do all I can to be growing my feathers
and my wings.

—Attar
Love Prayers

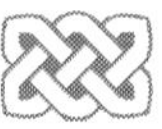

Take away me fear of death, Beloved One.
Fill me with the certainty of life that never ends.

OCTOBER 3

FEAST DAY OF SAINT GWEN TEIRBRON

Sweet White One,
fertile one, fruitful one,
bless, I pray, my life with your bounty.
May my life, like yours,
be abundant, rich with nourishment.
When adversity strikes,
may I, like you, remain faithful
to life's fertility,
its endless plenty.

—Meg Llewellyn
The Celtic Wheel of the Year

This sixth-century Welsh woman's name means "the white three-breasted one," and Celtic women called on her for help with infertility and breastfeeding.

OCTOBER 4

FEAST DAY OF SAINT FRANCIS

ANIMAL KINFOLK

Ancient Celtic Christians perceived
their loving relationships with animals
as signs of the Realm of God.
Animals are expressions of God's love and mystery;
interacting with them—whether as companion animals
or in the wild—helps us be more fully present in the moment.
They help us to recognize the interconnectedness of life.
They teach us compassion, and in the security
of an animal's unconditional love, we may be empowered
to recover that which is truest within us—
and find a new sense of identity and direction.
Animals show us God, but they are also our kinfolk,
connected to us by the strands of need and commonality
that unite all families.

—Kenneth McIntosh
Water from an Ancient Well

Thank you, Life-Giver, for the animals in my life.
May I learn from them about you,
about myself, and about love.

OCTOBER 5

YOU!

Do you know how beautiful you are?
I don't think you do.
But believe me, sweetheart,
there's a parade that marches out from you,
carrying a startling, secret song
that only you can teach the world.
You think you're ordinary,
but you can't see what the Beloved sees,
for you are wild, lovely, full of color and wonder.
Even if you can't see your heart's parade,
others will. Believe me. You are amazing.
So sing along with your heart, and I'll join in,
and together we will serenade
the Beloved.

—Hafiz

Love Prayers

Divine Lover, thank you for seeing
and calling into being the beauty of my true Self.

OCTOBER 6

LISTENING TO NATURE

Trees, like us, are energy vibrating as matter.
We vibrate as skin and bones and feet and brains;
they vibrate as bark and roots
and branches and sap.
Ask the natural world (the trees or the sea,
the prairie or the desert) to speak to you,
to tell you its stories. If you listen,
you may be called to provide healing
however and wherever you can.

—Melina Rudman
Sacred Soil

Teach me to truly listen, Life-Giver—to Nature,
to others, to my own heart, and most of all, to you.

OCTOBER 7

INNER SILENCE

As entering into this inner silence becomes a habit,
we become far more aware of the deviations
we habitually make from that tranquility.
Yes, things still happen in our day-to-day lives:
we lose the keys or we are late for an appointment;
we experience a sense of lack, or fear, or even depression.
But this plays out against the vast
backdrop of a deep inner silence.
Emotions become like the drama of heavenly bodies:
yes, stars explode, asteroids collide, nebula expand,
new stars form, but all this plays out against
the vast backdrop of an infinite space.
An infinite silence. A Divine silence.
In this silence we simply rest in the presence of God.
In silence, our inmost self comes home.

—Marc Thomas Shaw
Dante's Road

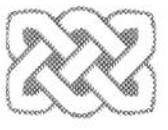

Show me the way, Spirit of Life, to make my home
in your Presence, in inner silence.

OCTOBER 8

HIDDEN RACISM

How can I discern my own inner racism, Lord?
Cleanse me, I pray, from my hidden errors in thinking.
Also, I ask that you restrain in me any intentional acts of racism.
Let not the habits of systemic racism rule my life.
Point out anything in me that is harmful to people of color,
and lead me into a new and better future.

—Patrick Saint-Jean, SJ
(based on Psalm 19:13,14 and 139:24)
The Spiritual Work of Racial Justice

Open my eyes, my mind, and my heart, Spirit of Love,
so that I see you present in all people.

OCTOBER 9

THE ONLY CONSTANT

Beloved,
from each of the world's subatomic particles
You created countless mirrors,
and each mirror reflects Your Face.
But reflections are fleeting.
If I want permanence,
I cannot seek to grasp at a reflection.
I must cling only to You,
the primal Source of all I see.
Why should I tear my soul apart over something
that is here one moment and gone the next?
You, Beloved, are the only constant
hidden within this world's transient beauty.

—Jami
Love Prayers

May my life be so rooted in you, Spirit of Love,
that this world's changes don't upset me.

OCTOBER 10

DIVINE NUDGES

I am not me when I do what others want me to do.
I am not me when I do what I think I *should* do.
I am only me when I act in accordance
with what my inner divinity nudges me to do.
My inner divine nudges are the actions of God within.
How do I discern that these nudges are from God?
When these nudges are accompanied
by feelings of inner peace, freedom, spaciousness,
excitement, joy, gratitude, and clarity . . .
then I know that their origin is God.
These feelings are indicators of God's presence.

—Rich Lewis
Sitting with God

Remind me, Loving One, to listen to my inner divinity,
rather than my need to please.

OCTOBER 11

TRUSTING GOD FOR BOTH NOW AND ETERNITY

I both saw God, and at the same time
I longed to see God;
I had God, even as I yearned for God.
This is the way our lives go;
this is the way they are meant to go while we are in this life.
God wants us to believe that we do in fact
see the Divine Presence continually,
even though we feel as though
we barely catch a glimpse of God.
Our belief fills our lives with grace.
In the end, God will be seen—and God will be sought;
God will give us rest now—
and God will be trusted for what we have in Eternity.

—Julian of Norwich
All Shall Be Well

When I cannot see you or feel you, Beloved One,
remind me you are still with me.

OCTOBER 12

MIND AND HEART

Thinking about abstract concepts like nondualism
can sometimes be a distraction
from experiencing all of reality.
When things get difficult or painful,
we may welcome something that shifts the focus
out of the heart and into the head.
Even here, there is a dualistic reduction.
We don't need to choose
between abstraction and concrete reality.
We don't need to live either out of the heart or our head.
Both are important. Together, synthesized,
they leads us further along our spiritual journey.
Separated, they can become tangents
that ultimately lead nowhere.

—Jeff Campbell
Discovering the Essence

May I explore your reality, Spirit of Life,
with both my mind and my heart.

OCTOBER 13

WOMAN WISDOM

Wisdom is yet another feminine image in the Bible
The concept of Wisdom as a woman was central
to the ancient Hebrews' thinking about God.
Sometimes, Wisdom is portrayed as a Divine consort,
a companion, a child, and as a feminine counterpart
to the Existing One, but within the Book of Psalms
and the Book of Proverbs, she is the Feminine Spirit,
rather than a Being separate from the Living One.
In the Bible, we hear the voice of Woman Wisdom,
the Feminine Spirit, calling us all—
regardless of gender—to follow Her path
to intimacy with the Living One.

—Lynne Bundesen
The Feminine Spirit

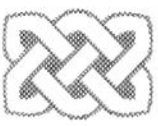

Spirit of Wisdom, show me your path.

OCTOBER 14

SEEING GOD ONLINE

God seeks beauty of holiness and wholeness
in our daily social media communications.
Mother Teresa believed the Living Christ was present
deep down in everyone,
especially those who distress and offend us.
These persons can be our spiritual teachers
challenging us to see the inner Divinity
that is often unknown to them.
In seeing Christ in the other—including the person
most unlike us or who pushes all our emotional buttons—
we are liberated to become God's healers in the world.

—Bruce Epperly
God Online

Help me, Spirit, to aways look beyond appearances
to see the Inner Christ.

OCTOBER 15

JESUS

Ultimately, it was Jesus Christ who brought me
to a new understanding of my spiritual path.
Because of him, today I call myself a Pagan follower of Jesus.
For me, Jesus exemplifies the unity
between the call to be actively involved in this world's struggles
and the call to be actively engaged in the spiritual world.
The Incarnation, God revealed in human flesh,
is a challenge to live the spiritual life
in fellowship with others—the "Body of Christ,"
the Incarnation as it's expressed
in the Earth's global community.

—Marjorie Bennett
Persistent Resistance

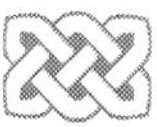

May I follow the example of Jesus, Spirit,
bringing Divine love to the community in which I live.

OCTOBER 16

PHYSICAL MOVEMENT

When you move your body,
your thoughts and emotions move as well.
You gain novel perspectives.
Your imagination is liberated.
So take your questions out for a walk.
Don't force the issue
or try to achieve something immediately.
Simply walk and let feelings and thoughts emerge.
It will be solved in the walking.

—Bruce Epperly
101 Soul Seeds for Healing and Wholeness

Move my feet and move my spirit, Spirit.
Let Your wisdom flow in and through me,
inspiring me to new ideas and new ways of living.

OCTOBER 17

DEATH AND RESURRECTION

Our own undoing—our times of greatest lostness,
failure, humiliation, or despair—
can be the most important and transformative moments
in our inner journey of awakening.
The powerful image Christianity gives us
is the death-resurrection journey of Jesus,
where we see the failure and humiliation of the cross
leading to new life and hope.
We have tended to theologize this
as something Jesus did on our behalf,
a transactional act of redemption that allows us
to remain passive recipients, rather than as something
that challenges us to actively undergo
a similar process of brokenness and resurrection.

—Sharon Grussendorff
Deeper

When all I see is death, remind me, Holy One,
that your resurrection power is always at work.

OCTOBER 18

THE SONG OF LOVE

The Infinite never stops playing Her flute,
for it is the Song of love.
When love refuses to be limited,
it reaches truth.
The fragrance of the Song spreads
everywhere, infinitely,
for nothing can stand in its way.
The Song gleams like a million suns,
and it sings what nothing else can sing:
the melody of truth.

—Kabîr
You're Already Home

Sing your song in my life, Spirit.

OCTOBER 19

SECURITY

As a mountain is firm beneath my feet,
so you, Lord, are a firm foundation.
My soul can rest in the security of you.
As the mountain goat finds surety
in the mountain beneath its foot,
so I find surety in you
You alone are my life's foundation.
On nothing else do I trust my foot to fall.
On nothing else do I establish my life.
Nothing is as secure as you, my Lord,
my God, my Rock.

—David Cole
Celtic Prayers & Practices

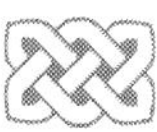

Living One, may my life be built
on your solid Rock.

OCTOBER 20

THE HUMILITY OF GOD

How would you feel if you heard God say
(as clear as your mother's voice was,
when you were very small),
"You are so lovely to Me that I have placed you
where I can always see you, as I would a rose"?
How would you feel if God knelt down
and said to you, "Forgive Me, my love,
for the pain you've felt, for the suffering
our separation has brought"?
How would you feel
if God tapped you on the shoulder, saying,
"I need you. You are My eyes, My hands, My legs, My voice.
Without you, I can do nothing"?
What would you do if God whispered in your ear,
"I am in debt to *you*, beloved one"?
Would you believe Him?

—Marietta Bahri Della Penna
Prayers of a Christian Sufi

Beloved, thank you.

OCTOBER 21

SUSTAINED BY THE INVISIBLE

Wipe the dust from my heart's mirror, Loving God.
As I go to work each day, as I follow my daily routines,
remind me not to rely on ego-strength.
You, the Hidden One within my heart,
give me all my skill and strength.
When I am successful,
may I not bask in my achievement,
for wins and losses come to everyone,
both streaming from Your grace.
Beloved One, my very existence comes from You.
The Invisible sustains me each moment of my life.

—Sa'di
Love Prayers

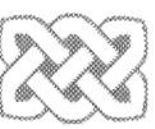

Hidden One, may I always seek your way,
rather than my ego's.

OCTOBER 22

HOPE AND TRANSFORMATION

Hope is a frame of mind that always looks forward,
that doesn't waste time looking over its shoulder at the past,
and it doesn't worry about what could have been—
but at the same time it doesn't insist on its own way.
It is open to the mystery of grace.
It's willing to be surprised. This is a hope
that makes the activist willing to be changed by the work,
to be transformed along the way.

—Marjorie Bennett
Persistent Resistance

Give me a hope, Life-Giver,
that's rooted in you.

OCTOBER 23

LEAVE IT WITH GOD

There are moments when
transformation and renewal elude us.
There are times when we cannot forgive
those who harass, traumatize, and abuse,
whether in ministry, family, or politics.
We need to leave forgiveness to God
when we can't forgive someone whose actions still distress us.
We need to trust God with the spiritual
and moral arcs of history
when we can't move them forward ourselves
due to our own fatigue, burnout, or trauma.
Still, God is at work in our lives to bring healing and wholeness
and give us the grace we need
to grow in and through life's challenges.

—Bruce Epperly
101 Soul Seeds of Healing and Wholeness

Loving Spirit, help me commit myself
to a life of renewal and creative transformation.

OCTOBER 24

PRAYER

If God connects all that is,
our intentions impact the whole of God's realm.
We don't pray to "the Big Man in the sky";
we pray as a part of the vast interconnected One
that includes ourselves
and reaches beyond the expanse of the cosmos.
And if that is so, then our prayers for others do matter.
To put it in ancient Celtic terms, prayers create "thin spots"
where the visible and invisible realms pass back and forth.

—Kenneth McIntosh
Water from an Ancient Well

Thank you, Spirit of Wonder, that I live in a world
that is both visible and invisible.
Teach me to live in both today.

OCTOBER 25

PORTALS TO INFINITY

Health and wholeness are a matter of perception—
a matter of seeing the Divine in yourself and others.
When the doors of perception are opened,
every face will be a portal to infinity.
Everyone will be Christ in disguise.
We will not be separate or superior.
We will honor our unity with every person and all creation.

—Bruce Epperly
101 Soul Seeds for Healing and Wholeness

Spirit of All Creation,
today may I see you in every face.
Let every encounter inspire me
to bless and be blessed.

OCTOBER 26

FLYING

Death cannot sever our connections
to the network of life—
because death is merely the pivotal moment
when we learn to fly.
Then, as we leap into the air—
naked, trusting only in the Creator—our wings unfurl,
ready to carry us into the Mystery that lies ahead.
As Sojourner Truth said as she approached her death:
"I am not gonna die, honey.
I'm going home like a shooting star."

—Patrick Saint-John, SJ
Home-Going

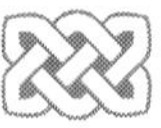

Thank you, Life-Giver,
that death is only the doorway into more life.

OCTOBER 27

SHADOWS AND SUBSTANCE

In the house of worship that is our body,
there's the danger of believing our outer projection,
the glittering image we present to the world.
In an age of fear, it is tempting to avoid introspection,
to cast our gaze away from our shadow self.
To remain true to our values,
to maintain the love that wins in the end,
we need to "wake up,
and strengthen what remains" (Revelation 3:2).
We need to value our true inner substance
over our desire to impress others.

—Kenneth McIntosh
Hope in an Age of Fear

Wake me up, Light of the World,
to my true inner being,
and help me let go of all that is false.

OCTOBER 28

PROTECTED

The Latin root words for *protect*
meant "to cover in front."
Imagine yourself holding one of the large round shields
that Celtic warriors carried. Behind this shield,
you are safe from the onslaught of the enemy's blows.
Although it cannot cover every piece of your body,
it covers your heart, the centermost part of you,
the inner core of who you are.
We are not immune to the dangers around us;
we will not magically be lifted above them.
And yet our innermost being is safe,
shielded by the One who loves us.

—Ellyn Sanna
Celtic Prayers for Times of Crisis

Shield me, Spirit, with your Presence.

OCTOBER 29

ALL-LOVING GOD

In contrast to images of divine power
as unilateral and coercive, today's global spirituality
sees God's power as all-loving and all-including.
Our Loving Parent doesn't horde power
or compete with humankind
but seeks to increase our personal freedom and creativity
in ways that complement the well-being of the whole,
as well as our own individual well-being.
God seeks abundant life for all of us.
God respects our freedom but works within
even our bad decisions to bring healing and illumination.

—Bruce Epperly
Become Fire!

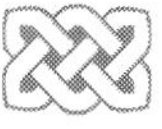

Thank you, Life-Giver,
for the humble generosity of your love.

OCTOBER 30

ETERNALLY CONNECTED TO GOD

Before my birth experience, I came from God,
and I will return to God.
I continue to evolve in my understanding
of my connection to my Source.
I evolve as I remain open to Spirit's presence
And my connection to others.
God's Presence is all pervasive and continuously creates.
Before my body existed, I was in God.
During my bodily birth, God released me into this world,
but He still wants me to remain connected,
with the hope of future intimacy and union.
Death will be a continued connection to God.

—Rich Lewis
Sitting with God

I came from you at my birth, Life-Giver,
and I know at death, I will only go deeper into you.

OCTOBER 31

HALLOWEEN

Gateway between this world and spirit world;
thin night, dark night, night of spirits;
night to remember those who have gone before.
I honor you, those whose blood I carry.
I welcome you;
may your memory guide me into truth.
Watch over your kin who walk this Earth.
Protect us and guide us.
Your blood runs in my veins, your spirits are in my heart,
your memories are in my soul;
bless us.

—Meg Llewellyn
The Celtic Wheel of the Year

Today is far more than a spooky children's holiday;
for the Celts, it was a joyful celebration of the reality
that death does not end our family ties,
that kinship survives even death.

NOVEMBER 1

SAMHAIN (ALL SAINTS DAY)

CLEAR REVELATION

Lord of the changing seasons,
of harvest time, frost, and hearth fire,
I thank You for this All Saint's Day morning.
The russet leaves fall thickly in the still, early light.
Like all the men and women who have ever lived,
they return to the Earth.
I thank You, Lord, for this moment in time,
this moment of clear revelation.
I thank You for the faith of my ancestors, remembered this day,
for Halloween candy, and pumpkin pie,
and the Communion of Saints, for cozy evenings
and the low-angled sun of a November afternoon.
In the name of the dead, I thank You!
In the name of the living, I thank You!
In the name of those to come, I thank You!

—Bill Palmer
Earth Afire with God

Samhain, as the juncture between
the two halves of the year,
is a holy and potent in-between time,
when the gate between the worlds swings open.

NOVEMBER 2

TIME TO HIDE OUT

After Elijah had riled the people of Israel,
the Living One gave Elijah a message
that said basically:
"Go hide out for a while until people
aren't as angry with you" (1 Kings 17:3).
Sometimes, it is better to retreat from conflict.
The implication here is that Elijah is to separate himself,
temporarily, from the political intrigue and conflict of his day—
and hide himself within the life-giving womb of the Divine,
beside the flowing waters of Creation.
God tells Elijah that his needs
will be provided for in this place.

—Lynne Bundesen
The Feminine Spirit

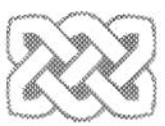

When I'm overwhelmed by the world's conflicts, Spirit,
remind me to hide myself in you, so I can be restored.

NOVEMBER 3

FEAST OF SAINT WINIFRED

HEALING AND PEACE

Blessed Winifred, holy peacemaker,
shaper of reconciliation, loving protector,
we ask that you grant healing,
to each of us who have been severed
from our sense of our own identity.
Heal those who bear the scars
of violence and violation.
Make us intact once more, whole and holy,
able to labor in your footsteps,
bringing peace, reconciliation, and protection
to all who are vulnerable, to all who have been broken,
to all who have been violated.
Help us to heal together in your blessed name.

—Meg Llewellyn
The Celtic Wheel of the Year

Winifred was seventh-century Welsh woman who suffered the trauma of sexual assault—and yet went on to be a strong leader of the church.

NOVEMBER 4

BE LIGHT!

Listen to me!
You no longer have to live within the box
that fear built.
But when you tell yourself lies,
you create your own prison.
You are carrying such a heavy load of desires;
how can you expect to float in the water of joy?
You are far too heavy.
Instead, be light.
Let it all go.
Keep only:
truth, detachment, and love.

—Kabîr
You're Already Home

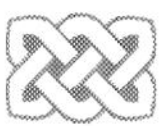

Help me, Beloved One,
to let go of everything that weighs me down.

NOVEMBER 5

THE BIRTHER

Infinite Birther,
thank You for moments of grace
in the unfolding life of the cosmos:
for the explosion of a star
and the creation of our solar system;
for the cooling aeons and the birth of our planet;
for the seed of life and the emergence of plants;
for the evolution of creatures
and the dawning of human consciousness;
for our ability to make a fire, a wheel, and a computer.
But far more than these all, we thank You for Yourself
and we celebrate Your creation.

—Ray Simpson
The Dance of Creation

Open my eyes today, Divine Birther,
to the wonders of Creation.

NOVEMBER 6

THE BODY OF JESUS

Jesus,
you are the resurrection and the life.
You are alive in our world, present in flesh and blood.
May I work to protect your living body,
present in all who suffer and are oppressed.
Give me eyes to truly see
and hands that are willing to touch.
Let no one be invisible to me.
Remind me, Jesus, that I need your entire Body,
not just the pieces that look like me.

—Patrick Saint-Jean, SJ
The Spiritual Work of Racial Justice

Help me, Loving Spirit, to see the living, broken Body that is your Presence on earth.

NOVEMBER 7

THE WILD GOOSE

Wild Goose, Holy Spirit of God,
release my life. Free my shackled heart.
Give me freedom to fly with you.
To love and to live in such fullness
that sky cannot be enough to hold me,
nor the highest heavens be too far to reach.
Eternal God of endless flight,
may I rise with you in freedom,
through the death and resurrection
of Truth and Life, Love and Son.
Give me a restored life,
both with the Divine and with humanity.
May I live in the freedom you offer, truly accepting it.

—David Cole
Celtic Prayers & Practices

Spirit of Freedom,
may I fly with you.

NOVEMBER 8

LOVING THE BELOVED

Every form I see is Your form, Beloved.
Every sound I hear is Your voice.
In each sweet scent, I breathe the perfume of Your Spirit.
In every word spoke to me, I hear Your voice, Beloved
In every touch, I feel Your hand.
Each kiss upon my lips is Yours.
Wherever I look, I see Your face.
Whomever I see, I see You.
Whatever I take, I take it from You
And then You remind me: it goes both ways.
When I speak, I am Your voice.
When I touch another in compassion, I am Your hand.
When I give my love away to anyone and anything,
I am Your love. And in each loving act I do,
I give You, Beloved, my love.

—Marietta Bahri Della Penna
Prayers of a Christian Sufi

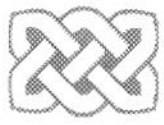

Today, Beloved Spirit, may I remember
I am your hands, your voice.

NOVEMBER 9

LAUGHTER

Want to hear a secret?
Laughter is simply this—the sound of God calling,
"Time to get up!"
It is the sun coming out from behind that cloud
you've been carrying over your head for way too long.
Laughter is the Light breaking open the ground
to build the structure of your real Self.
Laughter is the North Star, held steady in the sky
by the Beloved One, who is always saying,
"Yes, sweetheart, come this way. Come this way!
Come toward Love. Come toward Me.
Your feet already know the Dance.
Every cell in your body knows it too.
So come closer to Me."
What is laughter?
It is the song of a soul waking up.

—Hafiz
Love Prayers

May I laugh often today, Light-Bringer—
and hear your voice each time.

NOVEMBER 10

SEEKING AND SEEING

During this time that we suffer on Earth,
seeking is as good as seeing.
Leave your awareness of the Divine Presence up to God
in humility and trust, to reveal to you as God wants.
Our only job is to cling to God with total trust.
Whether we see God or only seek to see God,
I believe we add to the Divine Essence
when we simply fasten our minds and lives onto God.

—Julian of Norwich
All Shall Be Well

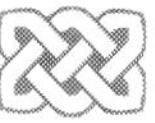

When I am frustrated
by my sense of your absence, Beloved,
help me to still cling to you.

NOVEMBER 11

THE TERRITORY OF HOPE

I've come to recognize that even the most painful death
always engenders a state of possibility.
Death vibrates through our lives and hearts,
opening up new spaces. While the Western eye
sees positive and negative space (or
foreground and background),
the African perceives no space as truly empty.
Seen from this perspective, the voids that death leaves
do not diminish us. They are not losses;
instead, they are places of possibility.
They offer us opportunities to learn and grow,
and in doing so, we expand rather than contract.
We move into the territory of hope.

—Patrick Saint-Jean, SJ
Home-Going

Show me, Life-Giver, the places in my life
where you are seeking to bring new possibilities
out of what I perceive as losses.

NOVEMBER 12

UNION WITH ALL THAT IS

Though on the surface we are still distinct and individual,
beneath the surface, we are part of all of it,
down to the smallest component.
This capacity to diminish our separate self-sense,
to loosen the ego's hold on us, to make room
for Divine love and wisdom to flow through us,
is the transforming union.
This is the closest possible identification with God
we can have in physical form.
It is paradoxically to become who we fully are.
As Christ says, "If you try to hang on to your life,
you will lose it. But if you give up your life
for my sake, you will save it."

—Marc Thomas Shaw
Dante's Road

Spirit, bring me into union with you and with all Creation,
that I might find my true Self.

NOVEMBER 13

DELIVER US!

My prayer to you, O Lord, is that at your time of favor,
the time you have chosen to act,
in the abundance of your love and kindness,
you will bring your deliverance and truth.
Pull our world out from the muck and the mud.
Don't let us sink.
Deliver us from the deep waters of hatred.
Do not hide from us.
We are in trouble, Lord. Hurry to help us.
I know I have failed you and your people again and again.
My guilt breaks my heart.
In humility, in pain, I ask you to heal me,
so that I can be a lens for your love,
shining your light into the world.

—Patrick Saint-Jean, SJ
(based on Psalm 69:13,14,17,19,20,29,30)
The Spiritual Work of Racial Justice

Help me, heal me, Deliver.
Shine through me.

NOVEMBER 14

THE MIRROR OF GOD

Oh Beloved One,
You have made the entire world as a mirror.
Within each atom You hid a hundred suns.
In each drop of water flows all the Earth's oceans.
When I look at a speck of dust, I see a thousand living things.
A gnat and an elephant are siblings.
In each grain of wheat is stored a hundred harvests.
An entire world exists in each seed,
and every insect's wing is a sea of life.
You hid Heaven in the pupil of my eye.
The core of my being is so small,
but You, Lord of all the worlds,
are living there.

—Mahmud Shabistari
Love Prayers

May I see you today, Giver of Life,
reflected everywhere.

NOVEMBER 15

NO NEED FOR FEAR

There is nothing in this world I need to fear.
Wherever I go, God is with me.
When I don't know how I will complete
the multiple tasks at work on time,
I know God will be there.
When I nervously await test results at the doctor,
I know God will be with me.
When a close friend or relative passes away and I grieve,
I know God will be with me.
When I am afraid to try something new, God will be with me.
Because I am a divine being,
when I move forward, I know all will be okay.
This knowing gives me confidence and freedom.

—Rich Lewis
Sitting with God

Thank you, Spirit of Love, that I can face
whatever this day brings—because
you are always with me.

NOVEMBER 16

UP, DOWN, FORWARD, OR IN CIRCLES?

Mature spiritualities speak of "descending."
Others describe a spiral dynamic.
This of course, might lead us to wonder,
"Am I meant to go downward?
Or in continual circles?"
Actually, it's even more complicated than that.
Our society's view that progress occurs
only in a straight line is overdone.
But it is not completely wrong.
There are places and times we should never return to again.
Sometimes, progress is forward. Or up.
Welcome, friends, to another opportunity
to practice radical nondualism.
Am I meant to descend? Travel in circles?
Take a straight line up?
Yes.

—Jeff Campbell
Discovering the Essence

Keep me open, Beloved One,
to the never-ending mysteries of following you.

NOVEMBER 17

ENDINGS AND BEGINNINGS

Great One, God of life and love,
as we stand at the edge of winter,
our fields are bare and empty;
the trees stand sleeping; our hearts turn inward,
and the world's fabric grows thin.
Remind us that what seems now to be ending,
is only the beginning of something new,
though it lies outside our sight.
The seed must die, the earth must sleep,
and trees must stand bare and silent,
before new life can come.
We too must die before we can be reborn.
This day of darkness is but the dawn of something new.

—Meg Llewellyn
The Celtic Wheel of the Year

Give me the courage to die, Spirit of Life,
so that I may be reborn.

NOVEMBER 18

BE STILL!

Discovering God online involves
pausing long enough to still
the constantly moving monkey mind
and the knee-jerk "gotcha" response,
in order to claim our freedom to respond
from a place of peace, reconciliation, and healing.
Like Elijah, we need to retreat long enough to transcend
the maelstrom of diverse and divisive voices.
In the spirit of Psalm 46, we need to "be still,"
making room for God.

—Bruce Epperly
God Online

Loving One, remind me to seek your stillness,
so that I may always respond to others
with grace and humility

NOVEMBER 19

THE TRANSFORMATION OF GRACE

Our human tendency is to try to improve ourselves,
to will ourselves to be better by being other than we are,
a more perfect version of ourselves.
Meanwhile, God's grace is the most effective way
to transform the stuff we are made of,
including our greatest "flaws,"
turning them into our most precious gifts.
This is the difference between true inner transformation
and our own attempts at creating outer change
through sheer self-discipline and willpower.
Inner transformation is a profound and mysterious process
we surrender to (as opposed to our attempts
to fix our skewedness using the same skewedness,
leading to even worse skewedness!).

—Sharon Grussendorff
Deeper

Help me, Birther,
to surrender to your transformation.

NOVEMBER 20

PRAYER FOR THE EARTH DURING CLIMATE CHANGE

We pray, O Three-in-One,
for a world of rising temperatures, drought and flood,
wild weather and broken seasons,
failed crops and dying forests.
Creator God, in Your mercy,
renew this damaged world.
For each creature threatened by climate change,
we pray, O Three-in-One.
Creator God, in Your mercy,
renew this damaged world.
You who made the Earth, remake her now.
Give us love and strength to partner with You
and renew this damaged world.

—Ellyn Sanna
Celtic Nature Prayers

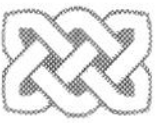

Give me the courage I need, Spirit,
to face the urgent crisis of climate change
and the wisdom to take action.

NOVEMBER 21

TOGETHER

We are stronger together.
Together, we can work
to infuse the ordinary visible world
with the presence of Divine Love.
Together—introverts and extroverts,
hermits and agitators,
visionaries and pragmatists—
we can change the world.

—Marjorie Bennett
Persistent Resistance

May I join hands with others, Divine Love,
so that with your help,
we can change the world.

NOVEMBER 22

SOUL DARKNESS

Dark nights of the soul, I know now,
would not be truly dark
if we could see the way out of them.
We must reach the point
where we believe the darkness will last forever.
We must allow ourselves
to be content with darkness, to accept it.
We must finally let go of our insistence
that we *deserve* light. We must surrender.
And there at last, to our surprise, God's will
coincides with our own deepest desires.
We step into the light,
and the Divine voice and our own become one.

—Marietta Bahri Della Penna
Song of a Christian Sufi

Beloved, may I find peace in the dark times,
knowing you are there.

NOVEMBER 23

ULTIMATE REALITY

Why argue about whether
Divinity is beyond all—or in all?
If you see everywhere as your home,
no pleasure or pain will fog your perception.
In that place of constant belonging,
Ultimate Reality is continuously revealed.
Light is Divinity's garment,
and the same light on which God sits
rests also on your head.
True God is all Light.

—Kabîr
You're Already Home

Today, Spirit of Light, may I be more aware that you live both within me and beyond me.

NOVEMBER 24

ALL I NEED

I've fallen in love with You, Beloved,
and now You've stolen me from myself.
You are all I need, all I crave.
Even if I die,
even if there were nothing left of me
but ashes,
I'd sing out from my grave:
You are all I need,
You are all I crave.

—Yunus Emre
Love Prayers

May I fall ever more deeply in love
with you, Beloved Spirit.

NOVEMBER 25

THE COSMIC CHRIST

Love and Creation vigorously move and unfold.
God wants us to revel in them.
She also wants us to participate.
We open ourselves and let the Christ act through us,
so that we become the hands and feet of this Love and Creation.
We become its voice.
Everything we touch embodies the Cosmic Christ.
When the veil of prime-time drivel
and cotton candy is lifted, we see: everything is holy.
This changes how we treat each other
and the Earth we inhabit.
I am on a lifelong journey of continuous discovery.
I want to continue to discover and mirror the dynamic unity
of the human Jesus and the Divine Christ
in my prayers and actions.

—Rich Lewis
Sitting with God

May I embody the love of Christ today and every day.

NOVEMBER 26

GRATEFUL

I am grateful, Spirit of Light, for all I have been given.
And yet I sorrow, Spirit of the Fire, for all that I have not.
Remind me that if I have less than some,
I have more than others,
and regardless, I am blessed.
I am grateful for my family, for the people who love me.
I am grateful for my home, for the walls that shelter me.
I am grateful for my friends, those who understand me.
I am grateful for my enemies, those who challenge me.
I am grateful for the animals who surround
me with their small lives.
I am grateful for the Earth, who gives me life.
I am grateful for the Spirit, who gives me joy.

—Meg Llewellyn
The Celtic Wheel of the Year

In this season of thanksgiving,
may I be truly grateful, Joy-Giver,
for all you have given me.

NOVEMBER 27

BECOMING GOD'S MESSAGE

Great Creator of the gleaming moon
and falling stars;
Great Saviour of the miraculous birth
and rising from death;
Great Spirit of the seers
and sacred words:
come into our minds, come into our mouths,
until we become Your message and sign.
Teach us to celebrate the beauty of Your creation
with truth and honor and justice.

—Ray Simpson
Dance of Creation

Today, Great Spirit, may I be your message,
a sign of your love to everyone I encounter.

NOVEMBER 28

ONE

Lord, grant me the grace to always receive you
as the ONE who lives within me.
Lord, open my eyes to see you as ONE
in me and in everyone.
Lord, thank you for coming to meet me where I am,
and bring me back where you want me to be.
Open my eyes to seeing you in my community as ONE.
Lord, give me courage to recognize the times
when I resist being ONE with you.
Lord, help me to see the shortcomings
that take me away from seeing you in everyone as ONE.

—Patrick Saint-Jean, SJ
The Spiritual Work of Racial Justice

Take from me, Spirit, anything and everything
that keeps me separate from you
and from the larger community in which I live.

NOVEMBER 29

GOD'S LOVER

Standing by the Beloved's side,
reach out to this world. Offer the comfort
you have drawn from the bottomless lake of Truth and Love.
Don't turn your back on the Earth's faltering steps.
The Earth needs you to be her lover,
your mouth open and sweet against her skin.
Make love to her rivers and seas,
to her furred creatures and feathered ones,
to those who gleam with scale and fin,
and to humans who are bleeding,
desperate for the Beloved's touch.
Be the hands of the Divine.
Be an open mouth against your lover's skin.

—Hafiz

Love Prayers

May I carry your love with me today, Holy One.

NOVEMBER 30

TRUE SELF

Who is my true self?
My true self is calm, content, and unafraid.
It is filled with life. It experiences God's love.
But to become my true self is very difficult
and requires ongoing struggle.
I need to fall out of my ego-self
into my true self. When I die to ego-self,
I awake to my true vocation.
I become the self God intended me to be.
The core of my true self is a deep knowing
that I am beloved and cherished by God.
That is who I am.

—Rich Lewis
Sitting with God

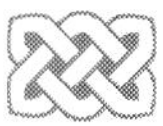

Help me, Life-Giver, to let go of all that is false,
so that I may become all that is real.

DECEMBER 1

ADVENT PRAYER

Lord of the shortening day,
of the snowflake, the fir tree, and the ice-rimmed lake,
be with me in the dark and cold of these four weeks.
The Faith of the prophets who foretold
His coming to a waiting world, be the Faith in me!
The Hope of the holy men and women
who longed for His coming, be the Hope in me!
The Love of His gentle mother
to whom He came in such humility,
be the Love in me!
In Faith, in Hope, in Love,
through these short, cold days of the early winter,
sustain me, O God, as I await Your coming!

—Bill Palmer
Earth Afire with God

In this season of Advent, Spirit of Love,
come into my life in new ways.

DECEMBER 2

THE CHRISTMAS STORY

When the Celts first encountered the Christmas story,
they readily opened their hearts and minds
to this tale of mystery and paradox.
It embodied the meaning they already celebrated
at the time of the Winter Solstices,
a time when the Yule log lit the darkness of winter
and celebrated the return of the sun's light and warmth,
when the holly and ivy symbolized the evergreen life
that endured even in cold and darkness.
For the Celts, the Christmas season was a "Thin Place,"
When the Holy Otherworld overlapped our everyday world,
filling even the ordinary with extraordinary meaning.

—Ellyn Sanna
Prepare the Way (introduction)

Today, in my ordinary life, may I see you, Life-Giver,
embodied in the deepest meaning of this busy season

DECEMBER 3

IN THE DARKNESS

In the darkness I turn to you.
In the shadow I turn to you.
As the darkness of the night surrounds me,
may I become aware of the dark night of my soul,
and the shadow within me.
Almighty God, bring me to the morning,
that I would know the rising light again.
Bring me to the dawning within my soul,
that I would know the rising of your Light
again within me.
Let me not despair
when I find myself in the darkness within myself,
but remind me that "even there you are also."
May I know your hand upon me,
drawing me always to the Light.

—David Cole
Celtic Prayers & Practices

When I'm tempted to despair, Light-Bringer,
remind me you are still with me.

DECEMBER 4

EMBODIMENT

Celtic spiritual guides saw God's light
shining in every newborn's face.
From this perspective, the light that shone
in the Bethlehem stable enlightens every human child
and shines more brightly as we grow
in wisdom and stature.
Following the footsteps of the Holy Child of Bethlehem,
we discover that the glory of God
is a fully alive human being, embodying
the Christ-like possibilities unique to every life.

—Bruce Epperly
Thin Places Everywhere

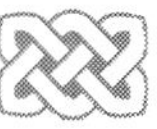

May I see you, Light of the World,
in every face I encounter today.

DECEMBER 5

GOD-WITH-US

The earth is becoming a wasteland:
Breath of the Most High, come and renew it.
Humanity is becoming a battleground:
Child of Peace, come and unite it.
Society is becoming a prison:
Key of Destiny, open doors to our true path.
The world is becoming a no-man's land:
God-with-us, come and make Your home here.

—Ray Simpson
Prepare the Way

Make your home, Spirit of Truth,
in my life.

DECEMBER 6

SAINT NICHOLAS DAY

SPIRIT OF GENEROSITY

Nicholas's generosity to the poor and hungry
is central to his story.
He was said to have spent
all his own fortune in good works.
He lived and died a simple servant
of God and his people.
After his death, Nicholas's story spread—
and he continued to work miracles
for those who called upon his help.
Today, the anniversary of Nicholas's death,
is still observed as his feast day.
The happy traditions of Saint Nicholas
can still enrich our lives.

—Bill Palmer
Santa Claus

Help me, Spirit of Generosity,
to follow in the footsteps of Saint Nicholas.

DECEMBER 7

THE HOLY JACK-IN-THE-BOX

God wants us to understand
that the sudden and joyful appearance of the Divine
in our lives will take us by surprise.
For the Divine works in hidden ways,
and yet at the same time, God wants us
to perceive the Holy Presence in our lives.
When this Presence comes to us,
it comes out of the blue, with such speed
that we are startled—and God wants us to trust
and wait for this Divine Jack-in-the-Box.
For God is utterly kind, and the Holy Presence
welcomes our hearts with total hospitality.
Blessed may God be!

—Julian of Norwich
All Shall Be Well

Give me strength and courage
to wait for the surprise of your Presence.

DECEMBER 8

WISDOM'S VOICE

In the Book of Proverbs,
Woman Wisdom calls out to us
not from temples or churches
but from places of human interaction,
the locations where people gather for business,
as well as all the ordinary spaces of human life
She is not shy or retiring as she speaks the truth,
and she does not work quietly behind the scenes.
Instead, she demands the dominion of her birthright
as the guiding force in all human affairs.
Her leadership creates a just society.
At Creation, She gave birth to the world,
and now she continues to make her home here.
She rejoices in life, and Her love and joy
are present everywhere, unspent.

—Lynne Bundesen
The Feminine Spirit

Teach me, Spirit of Wisdom,
to hear your voice more clearly.

DECEMBER 9

PRINCE OF PEACE

Christmas is the promise of tomorrow,
embodied in the adventures of today.
The Prince of Peace is born among us
and invites us on a holy adventure
in which we discover that love is stronger than fear,
reconciliation more powerful than hate,
and peace more enduring than violence.
Christmas asks us to choose a new way of life.
It calls us forward to horizons of hope and affirmation.

—Bruce Epperly
The Work of Christmas

Spirit of Peace, may I participate
in the meaning of Christmas today—
and every day.

DECEMBER 10

THE REAL SANTA

I propose that the spirit of Santa Claus—
even in the most crassly commercial exploitation
of his image—transcended the incredible excesses
of materialism. A sizeable segment of the population
still knew that Santa Claus didn't live at the mall,
that he judged us not by how much money we had,
but by how "nice" (as opposed to "naughty") we were,
and that his magic was about
the simple joys of Christmas morning
in your own living room, under your own Christmas tree.
Children—and the people who love them—
have always kept the real Santa Claus alive.

—Bill Palmer
Santa Claus

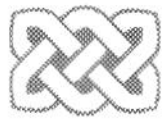

Life-Bringer, may I see you in Santa's image.
Keep the materialism and busyness of the season
from obscuring my awareness of your Presence.

DECEMBER 11

CHRIST IS COMING

You are holy, You are whole.
Let Earth give praise from pole to pole.
You are coming, coming here
to bring Your hard-pressed people cheer;
bringing to them human birth
born of heaven, born of earth;
bringing to them bread and wine,
giving hope of life divine.
You are coming, You are whole.
Let Earth give praise from pole to pole.

—Ray Simpson
Prepare the Way

Remind me today, Beloved One,
to seek your wholeness,
even in the brokenness of life.

DECEMBER 12

LOVING THE STRANGER

The foam-white Beloved came to us
without one home in all the world.
Tender and holy, He was driven into the cold.
Immanuel! A Stranger!
You angels of power, come down, come down!
Greet us! Show us!
Show us Christ in the stranger.
You Three of Power, kiss the cold stranger.
Hold his hand.
Warm his feet with the hair on your heads.
O! World-Pervading One!
O Jesu! O Mary! O Angels Three—
Michael, Gabriel, and Raphael!
Do not forsake the stranger to the winter cold.

—adapted from the *Carmina Gadelica*
The Celtic Wheel of the Year

In this holiday season, Beloved Spirit,
may I remember to see you—and serve you—
in the faces of those in need of physical security.

DECEMBER 13

HOLY ADVENTURES

The Celtic Christians recognized
that despite the apparent stability of ordinary life,
every day can be an adventure.
Our best laid plans can be turned upside down
by an unexpected phone call, chance encounter,
or synchronous event.
Daily adventures call forth a sense of the Holy
not just to protect but to inspire.
Christmas is an adventurous time,
and as we follow the wisdom of Celtic spirituality,
we will experience the vocation of every moment
and the beauty of each day.

—Bruce Epperly
Thin Places Everywhere

Open my heart and mind, Spirit of Adventure,
to new experiences and possibilities.

DECEMBER 14

MAGIC AND MIRACLES

The stories of Christmas invite us
to peer into the heart of God,
to discern the Divine in ordinary events,
and recognize that reality is always
more than meets the eye.
Christmas points to a magic reality—
a thin place—where miracles happen
and healings occur.
Christmas is the "impossible possibility"
that transforms our lives.

—Bruce Epperly
I Wonder as I Wander

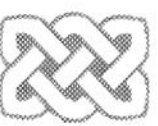

Heart of All Life, today remind to see
the true magic and wonder of the season.

DECEMBER 15

CHRISTMAS HOPE

Santa Claus, like Christmas itself,
continues to offer us something that truly transcends
our grown-up cynicism and disillusionment.
To fully embrace Santa Claus is to also
embrace the magic we knew through him as children.
To understand him is to acknowledge
his embodiment of the collective hopes and aspirations
of generations of our ancestors who created in him
a perfect symbol of both Christian virtue—
a loving generosity toward all—and the old solstice
celebration of life and joy in the darkest days of the year.
Santa is a myth that gives us hope.

—Bill Palmer
Santa Claus

Fill me, Light-Kindler,
with the hope of the Christmas season.

DECEMBER 16

IN THE DARKNESS

We wait in the darkness, expectantly, longingly;
come, O God Most High.
In the darkness, we see the splendor of the universe—
blankets of stars, the solitary glowings of the planets.
In the darkness of the womb, mortals are nurtured
and the Christ Child was made ready
for the journey into light.
In the darkness of dreams,
You spoke to Joseph and the wise ones
and You speak still to us.
In the darkness of despair and distress,
we watch for a sign of hope from the Light of Lights.
Come, O God Most High.

—Ray Simpson
Prepare the Way

Come, Light-Bearer,
to all the dark places in our world.

DECEMBER 17

INFINITY

We live in a God-filled universe
in which God is addressing us in every face
and each encounter. God is present
everywhere—and in its varied manifestations,
life is one, interdependent, and joined.
The Incarnation is God's invitation to experience God
in all things and all things in God.
The Incarnation opens the doors of perception
so that we experience Infinity
in chance encounters and unexpected places.

—Bruce Epperly
Thin Places Everywhere

Open my mental doors, Spirit, so that I
may see more clearly all the ways
you are incarnated in my life.

DECEMBER 18

CRADLE AND CROSS

In embracing both Christ's cradle and cross,
our souls expand to embrace the whole Earth.
Wherever we are, we are in God's presence.
We become Christ-like in our love for the world,
and we experience heavenly splendor
in the challenges of daily life,
as well as the promise of eternity in every encounter.
In simplicity of life, seeing God's presence
in ourselves and in our marginalized kin,
we become God's companions
in saving ourselves and the world.

—Bruce Epperly
Repairing the World

Show me how to be your companion, Spirit,
in the work of healing our world.

DECEMBER 19

THE BURNING HEART OF DARKNESS

Lord of Life, my heart is quiet, dark,
standing in the shadow of winter's cold,
of days of long darkness.
Have You left me here alone in the shadow of winter's night?
But, no, I hear You whisper. You have not gone,
but I have gone into the great womb,
a time of rest, of darkness of possibility yet unborn.
Here in the darkness, the spark of light still burns,
waiting for the spring.
Though You seem absent, though all is dark,
this is the time of new seeing, inner seeing,
visions of the unknown, and glimpses of God yet unguessed.
My soul is hidden from my sight,
but not from Yours, O great God,
Mother of Darkness and Father of Light.
This is but the veil that for a moment hides
Your burning heart.

—Meg Llewellyn
The Celtic Wheel of the Year

On this day when light is short and darkness long,
may I know the comfort of your Presence.

DECEMBER 20

THE POWER OF CHRISTMAS

This is the nadir of the natural year.
From the beginning, Christmas has combined
the Christian Church's commemoration of the birth of Jesus
with pre- and non-Christian customs
and rituals associated with celebrations at the Winter Solstice.
The age-old interplay between Christian joy
at the promise of redemption through the Incarnation
and Pagan-influenced celebrations of light and life,
feasting and revelry continues
to give Christmas its particular power.

—Bill Palmer
Santa Claus

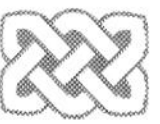

May I not be too busy today,
Spirit of Christmas, to celebrate your light.

DECEMBER 21

GOD WITH US

The Christmas stories show us God with us,
Fully immersed in the messiness of daily life,
in experiences of vulnerability and powerlessness,
at the mercy of heartless and uncaring political leaders.
The Incarnation brings heaven to earth,
and it brings earth to heaven.
A stable—and our own homes—become
chock-full with Divinity, and God is part
of the intricate interdependence of life,
feeling the full range of hope and fear,
touched by a child's cry as bombs rain down Ukraine,
or the grief of the parent of a teen
shot down in the city streets of America.

—Bruce Epperly
The Work of Christmas

Thank you, God, that you share
both the wonder and the ugliness of our lives.

DECEMBER 22

WINTER SOLSTICE

A FIRE IN THE DARKNESS

Warmth of all warmth, Comforter of all comfort,
Be within me this day.
I would share your warmth with others,
and be to the other that which the Great Other is to me.
Let not the darkness overcome us,
but let the light shine from within
to illumine that which is darkness.
As the darkness stretches its long hand over this land,
let your Light shine forth from within your people,
that none would be left in darkness,
but that instead we will live in the hope of the coming Light.
Great Light, be my guide.
Hold me fast in this present darkness,
that I may be the fire on a hilltop in this dark time.
Burn within me, now and ever more.

—David Cole
Celtic Prayers & Practices

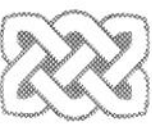

Shine through me, Light of All Life,
so that those who dwell in shadows
may see and be warmed.

DECEMBER 23

ARISE!

We arise today
in the deep formation of winter,
in the transforming power of ice,
in the cleansing work of frost.
We arise today
in the simplicity of the bare earth,
in the strength of the fierce elements,
in the beauty and brilliance of snow.

—Ray Simpson
Prepare the Way

In the beauty of winter, Beloved One,
may I discover strength.

DECEMBER 24

CHRISTMAS EVE

THE HEART OF THE INCARNATION

At Christmas, we discover
that the heart of the Incarnation
Is not about theological doctrines, moral guidance,
commandments, or dramatic revelations;
but the birth of a baby, an ordinary event
that has occurred several billion times,
which, in its simplicity, reveals God's relationship
with both humankind and the nonhuman world.
The Word and Wisdom of God,
the creative artistry of the universe,
and the energy of the Big Bang—
all take flesh in the vulnerability and innocence
of a newborn baby.

—Bruce Epperly
The Work of Christmas

May the wonder of your incarnation, Spirit of Love,
fill my life and flow through me to others.

DECEMBER 25

CHRISTMAS DAY

THE CHILD

Christ the King of Glory was born of human flesh.
See angels in the clouds, see messengers in the snow,
coming with speech and friendship for all humankind.
The Child of the dawn is born, Child of the clouds,
Child of the planet, Child of the stars,
Child of the rain, Child of the dew,
Child of the heavens, Child of the sky,
Child of the flame, Child of the dark,
Child of all spheres, Child of the moon,
Child of the elements, Child of the sun.
Child of God-Mind and Mary.
Christ is the first of all news, the best of all news.
Hey the Gift, ho the Gift
that came to us in winter.

—adapted from the *Carmina Gadelica*
The Celtic Wheel of the Year

Thank you, Child of God and humanity,
that you are born into our world, today and every day.

DECEMBER 26

JOY IN THE COLD

Why sorrow in the cold? Why tremble in the dark?
The soles of the King's feet have touched the Earth.
His Light has illumined the land.
His Light shines from the Earth, shines from the stars.
The plains glow to Him, the mountains glow to Him.
Soil and sea are illumined.
God the Lord of Heaven has opened a Door.
Christ of hope, Door of joy, Golden Sun in winter dark.
Hail to the Christ King, blessed is He,
who came to us in the dark and cold.
In time of change and fear, He is everlasting,
Without beginning, without end, for all ages, all time,
into the time beyond time.
Offer to the Being all your home;
include each stick, each stone, each rod and cloth.
Offer again all that you have—and let there be joy.

—Meg Llewellyn (adapted from an ancient poem)
The Celtic Wheel of the Year

Being beyond all being,
thank you for the open door into your Presence.

DECEMBER 27

DO YOU BELIEVE?

I choose to believe in Santa Claus.
He is wonderful and magical, and he remains, for me,
a messenger of the true meaning of Christmas.
He personifies a generous and jolly heart,
a tender love of children, a deep desire to help the poor,
and the holy mysteries of the cold and wintry Earth.
He urges us to be our best selves,
with the promise of enjoying the bounty of Creation
that sets our sights on the possibilities
of a more peaceful, generous, and happy world.

—Bill Palmer
Santa Claus

Now that Christmas Day has come and gone,
may the Spirit of Santa—the Spirit
of Divine Generosity—
continue to live in my life and heart.

DECEMBER 28

FEAR NOT

The angel said "fear not" to Mary and Joseph—
and angels continue to say "fear not" to us.
We are often afraid as we ponder the fate of the Earth,
observe the machinations of thoughtless
and heartless political leaders,
face our own inner demons, and worry about
the world our children and grandchildren will inherit.
And yet God's call is to believe the impossible,
to let go of our fears,
and give birth to the Christ Child in our time.

—Bruce Epperly
I Wonder as I Wander

Be born in me today, Divine Child
—and every day.

DECEMBER 29

GRACE THAT GIVES ITSELF AWAY

The word translated in many versions of the Bible
as "grace" comes from a Greek word, *charis*,
a feminine-gendered noun that carries the meaning
of "leaning toward," "freely giving oneself away,"
"reaching toward," "extending oneself to cross a distance."
This is a picture of the Feminine Spirit's
constant reaching out to Her unlimited Creation.

—Lynne Bundesen
The Feminine Spirit

Thank you, Spirit,
for all the ways you give yourself to me.

DECEMBER 30

INTOXICATING AND EXTRAVAGANT

The Jesus I was coming to know
was filled with magnanimity and abundance.
This Jesus rejoiced in his Father's providence;
he ate, drank, danced, and was shockingly extravagant.
His first miracle was at a party—a wedding—
where the host had run out of wine.
Jesus not only turned water into wine,
but he also made sure the new wine
was better than the previous one.
Did this story mean—could it possibly mean?—
that Jesus wanted to transform my colorless, tasteless life
into something rich hued and flavorful,
something intoxicating?

—Marietta Bahri Della Penna
Song of a Christian Sufi

Transform my life, Great Spirit.
I want to get drunk on you.

DECEMBER 31

NEW YEAR'S EVE

THE YEAR AHEAD

In the new year that lies ahead,
let us foster respect for each person
because God's image is in them.
Let us seek to relate
to that which is of God in everyone.
Let us listen for divine harmonies,
develop friendly creativity in our communities,
protect Nature, and bring back wonder
into science, learning, and even mundane jobs.
Let us foster inspired leadership
in business, politics, and media,
starting with ourselves.

—Ray Simpson
Prepare the Way

May the year ahead be blessed
with your light, Spirit of Love.

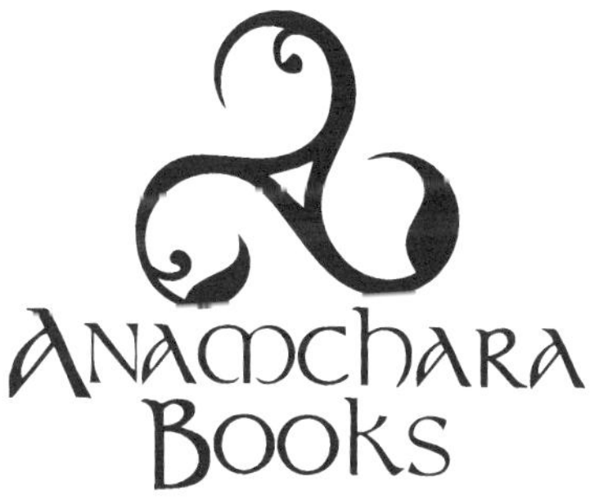

You can order any of the titles excerpted in this book from any online bookseller—or ask your local bookstore to order from our distributor, Ingram Content Group.

For bulk orders of 5 or more, contact
info@anamcharabooks.com
and receive a 50 percent discount off list price.

AnamcharaBooks.com

Printed in Great Britain
by Amazon